THE STEP-BY-STEP ASTROLOGY WORKBOOK

THE STEP-BY-STEP ASTROLOGY WORKBOOK

WHAT THE STARS WANT YOU TO KNOW

JESSIE ECCLES

Copyright © 2024 by Callisto Publishing LLC

Cover and internal design © 2024 by Callisto Publishing LLC

Illustrations by Shutterstock: © Nimaxs: cover (frame); © Sunflowerr: cover (zodiac signs); © Vasya Kobelev: interior (zodiac signs)

Art Director: Lisa Schreiber

Cover Designer: Matt Roeser

iStock/Getty Images: © Egor Suvorov: cover (night sky)

Art Producer: Maya Melenchuk & Stacey Stambaugh

Editor: Andrea Leptinsky

Production Editor: Emily Sheehan

Production Manager: Lanore Coloprisco & Martin Worthington

Callisto and the colophon are registered trademarks of Callisto Publishing LLC.

All rights reserved. No part of this book may be reproduced in any form or by any electronic or mechanical means including information storage and retrieval systems—except in the case of brief quotations embodied in critical articles or reviews—without permission in writing from its publisher, Sourcebooks LLC.

This book is not intended as a substitute for medical advice from a qualified physician. The intent of this book is to provide accurate general information in regard to the subject matter covered. If medical advice or other expert help is needed, the services of an appropriate medical professional should be sought.

Published by Callisto Publishing LLC C/O Sourcebooks LLC

P.O. Box 4410, Naperville, Illinois 60567-4410

(630) 961-3900

callistopublishing.com

Originally published as *Astrology for You* in 2022 in the United States of America by Callisto, an imprint of Callisto Publishing LLC. This edition issued based on the paperback edition published in 2022 the United States of America by Callisto, an imprint of Callisto Publishing LLC

Printed and bound in China.

OGP 10 9 8 7 6 5 4 3 2 1

CONTENTS

INTRODUCTION vi

HOW TO USE THIS BOOK ix

PART I: UNDERSTANDING AND INTERPRETING YOUR BIRTH CHART — 1

Chapter 1: An Introduction to Astrology — 3

Chapter 2: The Building Blocks of Astrology — 13

Chapter 3: The Basics of Reading Birth Charts — 25

PART II: YOUR BIRTH CHART AND THE TWELVE HOUSES OF ASTROLOGY IN ACTION — 37

Chapter 4: The 1st House of Astrology: The House of Self — 39

Chapter 5: The 2nd House of Astrology: The House of Value — 49

Chapter 6: The 3rd House of Astrology: The House of Communication — 59

Chapter 7: The 4th House of Astrology: The House of Home — 69

Chapter 8: The 5th House of Astrology: The House of Pleasure — 79

Chapter 9: The 6th House of Astrology: The House of Health — 89

Chapter 10: The 7th House of Astrology: The House of Relationships — 99

Chapter 11: The 8th House of Astrology: The House of Sex & Death — 109

Chapter 12: The 9th House of Astrology: The House of Spirituality — 119

Chapter 13: The 10th House of Astrology: The House of Ambition — 129

Chapter 14: The 11th House of Astrology: The House of Friendship — 139

Chapter 15: The 12th House of Astrology: The House of Secrets — 149

A FINAL NOTE 158

RESOURCES 160

INDEX 161

INTRODUCTION

Professionally, I am an intuitive astrologer and educator. I am also a mom, wife, lifelong learner, world traveler, self-development junkie, and nature lover. I have been practicing astrology professionally since 2015, with two certifications, and have had the honor of profoundly impacting, validating, and supporting thousands of clients through my astrology courses and consultations.

I am a Leo Sun, Aquarius Moon, Sagittarius rising with an 8th house stellium. My Mars is in Virgo in the 9th house. In other words, I am here to teach you to shine out as the most authentic, unique version of yourself. I express myself and my teachings in a concise and relatable way. I'm not afraid of the darker parts of humanity and can hold space and offer realistic advice for people processing big emotions.

Astrology has been part of my life since a young age, when my Leo self was obsessed with learning everything I could about—well, me. I loved horoscopes, Myers-Briggs, numerology, and anything I could find that gave meaning to my life. I've also always enjoyed connecting with others and helping people through their own journeys, which is why I decided to pursue a bachelor's degree in education and a master's degree in international education and intercultural relations. Though I had the benefit of achieving advanced degrees and an early career I was passionate about, I always had a deeper knowing that there was more to life than school and working. I spent years traveling the world in search of something greater than myself, only to return home to find that everything bigger than myself is inside and that astrology is a way to give meaning to that inner knowing.

Learning the language of the stars became a mirror for my own life. As I began tracking my own astrological cycles and using them to plan my next steps, I quickly realized how impactful and meaningful astrology is. Now, as an astrologer, my focus is to teach others to see what the stars want them to know—how to open up their own potential, validate their unique gifts, support themselves through life's lessons, and come back to their own intuition. My goal is to empower others to be the best version of themselves by using a practical approach that is easy to digest and practice in real life.

I do this work because I know it works. Astrology has helped my clients find the clarity they need to feel validated in their life path and get clear on future steps time and time again. I've had clients start or end careers and relationships, make life-changing relocation decisions, and heal and integrate lifelong patterns and wounds.

While this workbook will support you through life transitions and a range of complicated feelings, any ongoing or debilitating feelings of depression or anxiety should be addressed by a medical professional. This book is not a replacement for a therapist, medication, or medical treatment.

As you'll learn in this book, astrology is one of the oldest and most accurate tools used in human history. It brings your unconscious to your consciousness and illuminates your highest path forward. I am grateful to be part of your journey.

HOW TO USE THIS BOOK

This is a step-by-step interactive workbook applicable to all astrological signs. It is written for all levels of astrology knowledge. You will need your astrological birth chart, calculated using your birth date, time, and location. If you need help accessing this, there is a section in the book that provides easy-to-follow instructions to help you easily obtain your birth chart at no cost to you.

There are two parts to this book. The first part lays a foundation for astrology basics. If you have little astrology knowledge, this part is especially important in getting the most out of the second part of the book. The second part has twelve chapters, each one focusing on one of the astrological houses, that each contain five astrology-based workbook exercises.

The book is designed to be worked through in the order in which the chapters and exercises are laid out. Each chapter focuses on an individual house in your birth chart, each of which represents a different area of human life. You may find that one area of life, such as relationships or career, feels most relevant to you at this time, and you are welcome to skip to that section if it will be most beneficial. The astrological houses are in order for a reason, though, in that each area of life builds on the former house. Because of this, it is recommended that you work through every chapter and exercise to understand your full astrological birth chart.

PART I

UNDERSTANDING AND INTERPRETING YOUR BIRTH CHART

Astrology is a study of the stars used to understand human nature. For centuries, cultures around the world have used the changing seasons and the movement of the planets from Earth's perspective as a way to discern the meanings of life cycles and human experiences. Humans are complex, though. It is no wonder that astrology is a nuanced system with a complicated history.

In this first part, you will learn astrology's origins, ancient and modern systems and applications, key components of astrology, and how to use the foundations of astrology to interpret birth charts. Though it may seem far-fetched to actually be able to read a birth chart, by learning the foundations of astrology and its building blocks, you'll find this ancient study much more accessible for day-to-day life.

The goal is for you to understand enough about the background information and building blocks of astrology to apply its study to your personal life. It won't take you long to realize that astrology can support you on your journey of self-discovery and guide you to making empowered decisions and ultimately living your most authentic, aligned life.

CHAPTER 1

AN INTRODUCTION TO ASTROLOGY

Astrology is an ancient tool that has been used for centuries for self-reflection and to make major decisions and future predictions. Today, though astrology is no longer considered a science, it is experiencing a surge in popularity, likely as a result of its obvious connection to personal growth and development. In this chapter, you will learn what astrology is, its historical context, the different astrological systems used today, and the benefits of studying it for personal growth.

During times of stress, change, or confusion, many people look for external guidance. As astrology has gained in popularity more recently, it is not difficult to come across incorrect or incomplete information about the complex study and interpretation of the stars, which is not helpful when you are already at a low point. This chapter will provide clarity around any misconceptions and myths, and it will show that you are supported by the signs, which can reveal to you how to live your most authentic life.

Though you could easily spend a lifetime studying the depths of astrology, there are many aspects of it that are accessible, easy to learn, and applicable to your daily life. Understanding the context of astrology can support you on your journey of self-discovery and guide you through life's challenges.

WHAT IS ASTROLOGY?

Astrology is the study of the influence that celestial bodies have on human lives. Astrologers use the positions of the planets to make interpretations for two main purposes: to explain or predict current events in the collective and to provide insight into an individual's innate characteristics.

Historically, astrology was considered a science. It was commonly accepted across society and was even a respected academic discipline. Astrologers were highly regarded and sought out by leaders to make decisions based on the positions of the planets. Today astrology is not considered an exact science, like astronomy, but is instead used to support you in understanding yourself, your characteristics, and your life patterns.

While many astrologers today do make future predictions about the continued developments in society, astrology is especially useful as a bridge to understanding yourself more deeply. It can support you in understanding your emotional body, the way your mind processes information, what you value, how you want to feel loved, and so much more.

You probably know your zodiac sign, which is also known as your Sun sign. In the context of astrology, the Sun is one of ten planets, each located in one of twelve zodiac signs. (The Moon is also considered a planet for astrological purposes.) You may or may not resonate with the description or the horoscope of the placement of your Sun sign. That is because on its own, its meaning is too simplistic. Astrologers need the date, time, and location of your birth to produce your full astrology chart. The planets and signs, combined with other influences such as houses, aspects, elements, and modalities, form a more complete story of who you are.

THE DIFFERENT ASTROLOGY SYSTEMS

Most human civilizations saw a link between the positions of the planets in the sky and the cycles of human life. Historically, numerous cultures have formed an astrological practice and unique astrology system. Today, there are two astrology systems practiced most commonly: Western (Tropical) astrology and Vedic astrology.

Vedic astrology comes from the Vedas, the oldest texts of Hinduism. Karma is the central theme of Vedic astrology. Vedic astrology uses the sidereal system, which is based on each planet's connection to the constellations in relation to Earth. Since Earth is on an axis, the planets' locations in relation to the constellations and Earth change over time. This means, according to Vedic astrology, if you think you are an Aries—no, you aren't. Your zodiac sign today would actually be different than what you think, because Vedic astrology uses additional constellations beyond the twelve you know, and their relation to Earth changes over time.

Western astrology, which is the system this workbook uses, centers on the relationship between Earth and the Sun. It measures the closeness of the Sun to Earth's Tropic of Cancer and Tropic of Capricorn. This is why it is also known as Tropical astrology. While Western astrologers do use the twelve signs based on the constellations' positions relative to Earth, Western astrology is actually based on the seasons. In the northern hemisphere, Aries begins on the spring equinox, Cancer on the summer solstice, Libra on the fall equinox, and Capricorn on the winter solstice.

ASTROLOGY AND ITS MODERN APPLICATIONS

Throughout history, astrology has had periods of great acceptance, when it was even practiced by astronomers and doctors. It has also had periods of decline, when varying religions and scientific discoveries dominated. Though astrology has been used as a tool for self-discovery for centuries, it is experiencing a surge in popularity in the twenty-first century.

It is likely that the recent rise in popularity of astrology is tied to an increased interest in wellness. Over the last several decades, the wellness industry has exploded, not just around physical health but also around mental and spiritual health. Since astrology is a tool to better understand yourself on a deeper level, there is an obvious connection to having it support your mental and spiritual well-being.

In addition, aspects of astrology can be very lighthearted and easy to share and engage with on social media. This is why so many more millennials and members of

An Introduction to Astrology 5

Gen Z are looking for their birth times. It is a way to connect with others who have similar astrological traits or playfully tease those who differ from you.

Beyond astrology's link to individual wellness, astrologers also use it as a tool to predict the future. In the twenty-first century, humans are used to having access to information in a split second. More than ever, we are uncomfortable with the unknown, ambiguity, and uncertainty. Astrology can be used as a tool to provide some clarity and insight into what the collective, or you as an individual, may expect to experience in the future.

COMMON MYTHS AND MISCONCEPTIONS

1. Astrology is fortune-telling.

   Astrologers do not have a crystal ball or claim to be able to pinpoint your exact future. Though there is a meaningful relationship between the positions of the planets and humans that can help you navigate life, astrology is not fatalistic and should not be used as a reason that your life is or isn't a certain way.

2. Astrology is a religion.

   Astrology is not a belief system and has never been incorporated in a system of worship. It is the study of the influence that celestial bodies have on human lives and is practiced by astrologers to help provide guidance on current events and help you navigate daily life.

3. Astrological zodiac signs are the same as astronomical constellations.

   Zodiac signs and constellations are not the same. Different astrology systems, such as Vedic and Western astrology, use different zodiacs. When Western astrology was created, many of the same names from constellations were used for zodiac signs based on general location, but zodiac signs are not exact markers in the sky.

The Step-by-Step Astrology Workbook

4. Astrology is just generalizations.

    Horoscopes are general, but astrology is not. Since horoscopes are the most easily accessible way to approach astrology and they outline only twelve options for the entirety of the human experience, astrology initially appears to be general. As you will learn in this book, astrology is much more than your Sun sign.

5. There is a thirteenth zodiac sign.

    There is an additional constellation between Scorpio and Sagittarius, but it is not part of the system that Western or even Vedic astrology uses. This is used in constellation astrology.

ASTROLOGY FOR PERSONAL GROWTH

Through your birth chart, you are able to see the different characteristics of your nature, personality, and psyche; how they express themselves; and what areas of your life are influenced by these traits. This information is all accessible when you understand and are able to interpret the meanings of the planets, signs, and houses in your birth chart. The planets all represent different characteristics of your nature, personality, and psyche. The zodiac signs under which these planets are present in your chart indicate how those characteristics will express themselves, and the houses in which these planets are located in your chart represent what area of life is influenced. Since all parts of the human experience are present in your birth chart, you have the opportunity to explore the depth of who you are and how you experience life.

Not only does understanding your birth chart give you the opportunity for self-discovery and help you align with the most authentic version of yourself, it can also support you in feeling validated by some of your more challenging experiences as it leads you to understand your life lessons and how to best process and overcome them.

As you prepare for your future, understanding your birth chart and current life cycles can be a catalyst in supporting you living your most authentic life path.

An Introduction to Astrology   **7**

Embrace Self-Reflection and Self-Discovery

Your birth chart can put into words things you may already feel intuitively. Society may tell you that you are or should be a certain way, but understanding your birth chart can put you on a path of true self-discovery. For example, you may be told that you are too direct, but then find out that you are a fiery Moon in Mercury speaking to a sensitive water sign. Understanding this creates opportunities for self-reflection and opens conversation around your differences. Through reflecting on each piece of your birth chart and therefore each of your innate characteristics, you may find a deeper appreciation for yourself and others.

Explore Your Most Authentic Self

Everyone wants to live a life of authenticity, but few really know their most authentic self. Your birth chart is a cheat sheet in getting to the core of your inner self. Your most authentic self isn't simply your job, your partner, or your material possessions. It is much deeper than that. Being your most authentic self means being consistent in the way that your values, needs, thoughts, words, and actions align. Understanding your birth chart can give you insight and a deep appreciation of each of these aspects in your inner core that are unique to you.

Uncover Pathways Through Life's Trials

Life is complex, challenging, and often confusing. If everyone knew exactly why they are here on Earth and had clear steps to get there, avoiding any lessons along the way, it might feel pretty pointless. Your birth chart highlights unique lessons that you will experience—and need to experience—as part of your journey to your highest potential. Your chart also gives insight on how you are actually the best person equipped to handle these very lessons through unique self-care tools and coping strategies. Understanding your birth chart isn't a means to avoid life's trials; rather, it is a way to be prepared for and supported through them.

Discover Your Compatibility with Friends, Family, and Partners

There are certain types of personalities you likely get along with easily, and others that challenge, trigger, and frustrate you. Understanding both your birth chart and the other person's birth chart, whether they are your friend, family member, or romantic partner, can give you the key to unlocking where you are aligned and where there may be more challenging differences. The best way to make these types of interpretations is by pulling a synastry chart or a composite chart. These charts will show your compatibility in all areas of life, such as emotions, communication, and values.

Prepare for Your Future

Your natal birth chart does not change. It will show you your innate characteristics, core desires, and life lessons. The planets in the sky are always moving, influencing the collective and your individual birth chart in a unique way each moment. By looking at the current planetary movements, or transits, you can learn what cycles you are moving through over certain periods of time. As you move through major life decisions or times of uncertainty, this can be particularly supportive in helping you understand current priorities, have a clear picture of your options, and make the most authentic decisions for your future.

An Introduction to Astrology　　**9**

KEY TAKEAWAYS

In this chapter, you learned what astrology is, its historical context, the different systems used today, and the benefits of studying astrology for personal growth. Understanding the context of astrology can support you on your journey of self-discovery and guide you through life's challenges.

◆ Throughout history, astrology has been considered a scientific and academic discipline. Astrologers were once highly regarded and were sought out to predict future events and understand an individual's innate characteristics.

◆ Astrology is not a religion, fortune-telling, or simple generalizations. It is the study of the influence celestial bodies have on human lives. Astrologers use the positions of the planets to predict current events and help you navigate daily life.

◆ Though astrology is not considered a science today, it is useful in supporting you in understanding yourself more deeply through self-reflection practices.

◆ Astrology can help you understand your compatibility with others, giving you the key to unlocking where you are aligned and where there may be more challenging differences.

◆ Your birth chart represents all parts of the human experience, helping you understand your most authentic self, including your life lessons, so that you can make aligned decisions both in the present and for your highest potential in the future.

CHAPTER 2

THE BUILDING BLOCKS OF ASTROLOGY

Astrologers spend years studying the depths of astrology. However, there are many aspects of the study that are accessible and easy to learn for those who are not professional astrologers, and even better, these things are applicable to your daily life. Understanding the building blocks of astrology can help you discover how to live your most authentic life path.

In this chapter you will learn about the major players in astrology—the planets, signs, and houses. You likely know your zodiac sign, but reciting the qualities of each sign may not come naturally to you. This chapter helps break down the unique characteristics of each sign by also identifying the elements, polarities, modalities, and orientations of each sign, putting together a full picture of why each zodiac sign is described the way that it is. You will also gain a basic understanding of the twelve houses, which is particularly important as you move into the later parts of the workbook.

Each of the twelve signs, twelve houses, and ten planets detailed in this chapter shows up in your birth chart in a unique way. Before you learn how to interpret these in your chart, it is important to have a foundation of each of these components to have a holistic understanding of astrology.

THE TWELVE ZODIAC SIGNS

The twelve zodiac signs are the foundation of astrology. You likely know your zodiac sign, or Sun sign, but you may not know that you have all twelve zodiac signs in your birth chart. Regardless of where your Sun sign and other planets are, it is important to have a basic understanding of the twelve signs and what area of your chart, or house, each is located in so that you can understand how their energy shows up for you.

Aries (March 21–April 19): The symbol is the ram. As a cardinal fire sign and the first sign of the zodiac, Aries is a born leader. Aries is direct and ambitious and loves competition.

Taurus (April 20–May 20): The symbol is the bull. As a fixed earth sign, Taurus is practical and stubborn and loves experiencing life through all five senses.

Gemini (May 21–June 20): The symbol is the twins. Gemini does everything in life as if there were two. As a mutable air sign, they are insatiably curious, communicative, and flexible.

Cancer (June 21–July 22): The symbol is the crab. As a cardinal water sign that is deeply emotional and connected to their intuition, Cancer is a born nurturer but can have a hard shell.

Leo (July 23–August 22): The symbol is the lion. As a fixed fire sign, Leo is passionate, loyal, creative, and playful; you always know when a Leo is in the room. They come across as having an ego, but they live from their heart.

Virgo (August 23–September 22): The symbol is the virgin. Everyone needs a Virgo in their life. As a mutable earth sign, Virgo is service oriented, organized, and practical, and can create a system for anything.

Libra (September 23–October 22): The symbol is the scales. As a cardinal air sign, Libra is the harmonizer of the zodiac. Libra craves balance and achieves it through collaboration and diplomacy.

Scorpio (October 23–November 21): The symbol is the scorpion. The Scorpio is the fieriest water sign. As a fixed water sign, Scorpio is intense and powerful. They are here to go deep and transform.

The Step-by-Step Astrology Workbook

Sagittarius (November 22–December 21): The symbol is the archer. The Sagittarius is the optimist of the zodiac. As a mutable fire sign, Sagittarius does everything on a big and expansive scale. They are on an eternal quest to grow.

Capricorn (December 22–January 19): The symbol is the sea goat. As a cardinal earth sign, Capricorn is known for their ambition and wisdom. Though it may take them longer to get there than others, they are destined for success.

Aquarius (January 20–February 18): The symbol is the water bearer. As a fixed air sign, the Aquarius is the most difficult to define, because they are a natural rebel. They are rebellious because they are dedicated to making humanity better.

Pisces (February 19–March 20): The symbol is the fish. As a mutable water sign, Pisces is the dreamer and believer. The last sign of the zodiac, Pisces is the most intuitive and sensitive.

WHAT IT MEANS TO BE BORN ON THE CUSP

If you are born a few days before or after the Sun changes zodiac signs, you may have been told that you are born on a cusp and therefore take on characteristics of both signs. This is incorrect.

Each zodiac sign consists of 30 degrees (0 to 29), creating the zodiac wheel of 360 degrees. If you have been told you are born on a cusp, it is probably because your Sun is either at 29 degrees of one sign or 0 degrees of the next. While this is unique in that it is a critical degree of the zodiac, it does not mean that you are a blend of both signs.

The Sun in your birth chart is only located in one sign of the zodiac, and you will take on characteristics of that particular sign. You may have other planets, such as Mercury or Venus, which are typically close to the Sun, or other activity happening in the next sign that could influence

continues >

The Building Blocks of Astrology

WHAT IT MEANS TO BE BORN ON THE CUSP *continued*

how you experience the other zodiac sign. This is why you may feel like you are a blend of both signs, but ultimately your Sun is only in one sign of the zodiac.

If you are someone who was born on the exact day the Sun changes zodiac signs, it is especially important for you to have your exact birth time. This will tell you in which sign of the zodiac your Sun is located and what qualities your natal Sun will take on in your birth chart.

SUN, MOON, AND RISING SIGNS

The Sun, Moon, and rising are considered the Big Three in your birth chart. While every part of your chart holds equal significance, understanding your Big Three alone can help you feel validated and empowered.

The Sun and the Moon are both luminaries, which means sources of light. They are rulers of day and night and are the most abundant sources of light on Earth. The rising sign is an imaginary point in the sky that is literally rising in the east at the moment of your birth.

You likely already know your Sun sign. This is your zodiac sign. It represents your life force, identity, ego, and personality. The Sun is the brightest object in Earth's sky, and in your natal chart it is how you shine and express your individuality. It also gives insight into how you need to feel revitalized and recharged.

Your Moon sign represents your emotional body. It is the subconscious part of yourself that you may typically keep hidden but that comes out during emotional reactions. It also gives insight into how you nurture yourself and others and what is needed for you to feel restored.

Your rising sign, also known as the ascendent, is the lens through which you see the world. It is how you approach life. It also represents your physical body, and therefore it can act as a shield to the outside world. The ascendent is crucial because it determines how the houses are laid out in your chart.

16   The Step-by-Step Astrology Workbook

THE FOUR ELEMENTS

Each of the twelve zodiac signs is associated with one of four elements found in nature: fire, earth, air, or water. Though each individual sign will have unique qualities, the elements are the foundation to understanding each sign.

The fire signs are Aries, Leo, and Sagittarius. Fire signs are passionate, impulsive, creative, and courageous. They typically have a sense of confidence and are not afraid to say what they think.

The earth signs are Taurus, Virgo, and Capricorn. Earth signs are dependable, practical, goal-oriented, and grounded. They are in touch with the five senses and appreciate material or tangible things in life.

The air signs are Gemini, Libra, and Aquarius. Air signs are intellectual, communicative, social, and curious. They love a stimulating conversation or good book and take a free-spirited approach to life.

The water signs are Cancer, Scorpio, and Pisces. Water signs are intuitive, nurturing, perceptive, and sensitive. They are typically private and feel connected to their home or value alone time.

In nature each of these elements is necessary for human life. They work together in harmony. Your birth chart may have a dominant or even a missing element, where most of your planets fall in one or two elements. Knowing your dominant element can help make sense of your overall chart and understand where you may be out of balance. You may find that you work well with or are attracted to others with the elements that are less dominant in your chart.

ASTROLOGICAL POLARITIES

The twelve zodiac signs can be divided into six sign polarities. This is where two signs sit directly opposite each other on the elliptic. The polarities represent positive and negative. This does not imply good or bad; they simply have different charges. Some astrologers will use terms like "yin and yang" or "active and receptive."

The Building Blocks of Astrology

The positive polarities are fire and air signs: Aries, Gemini, Leo, Libra, Sagittarius, and Aquarius. The negative polarities are water and earth signs: Taurus, Cancer, Virgo, Scorpio, Capricorn, and Pisces. Each polarity shares a modality and creates an aspect called an opposition, since they are 180 degrees apart.

The six zodiac sign polarities represent:

◆ Aries and Libra—the self versus the other. This axis is about autonomy and compromise.

◆ Taurus and Scorpio—form versus transformation. This axis is about values and acquiring wealth.

◆ Gemini and Sagittarius—the lower mind versus the higher mind. This axis is about searching for knowledge and truth.

◆ Cancer and Capricorn—private versus public. This axis is about our inner world and outward status.

◆ Leo and Aquarius—personal versus impersonal. This axis is about creativity and expression.

◆ Virgo and Pisces—physical health versus spiritual health. This axis is about how to be of service.

Each pair of signs in a polarity may seem like they do not have similarities, but they are really two sides of the same coin. In each polarity, you are meant to find balance. You may find that you work well with or are attracted to others with planets in the opposite polarity, especially the sign opposite your rising.

THE THREE MODALITIES

Each of the twelve zodiac signs is associated with one of three modalities: cardinal, fixed, or mutable. Modalities represent the sign's interaction with the outside world and speak to a particular behavioral style. Each modality consists of two polarities and will include one of each of the four elements.

Cardinal signs are Aries, Libra, Cancer, and Capricorn. Cardinal signs are the initiators of the zodiac. They start every season. In the Northern Hemisphere, Aries begins on the spring equinox, Cancer on the summer solstice, Libra on the fall equinox, and Capricorn on the winter solstice. Cardinal signs tend to be ambitious, opportunistic, and strong leaders.

Fixed signs are Taurus, Scorpio, Leo, and Aquarius. Fixed signs are the doers of the zodiac. They are in the middle of every season. In the Northern Hemisphere, Taurus is in the middle of spring, Leo in the middle of summer, Scorpio in the middle of fall, and Aquarius in the middle of winter. Fixed signs tend to be determined, purposeful, and dependable.

Mutable signs are Gemini, Sagittarius, Virgo, and Pisces. Mutable signs are the chameleons of the zodiac. They end every season. In the Northern Hemisphere, Gemini ends spring, Virgo ends summer, Sagittarius ends fall, and Pisces ends winter. Mutable signs tend to be versatile, adaptable, and personable.

Plans are created by cardinal signs, built by fixed signs, and perfected and evolved by mutable signs; all three categories are necessary in sustaining life. Your birth chart may have a dominant modality. If this is the case, it is likely that you work well with people who have strong placements in a different modality.

ASTROLOGICAL ORIENTATIONS

The orientations of the signs and houses are one of the ways in which an astrologer looks at an individual's approach to life. Each of the twelve zodiac signs and houses corresponds to one of three orientations: personal, social, or transpersonal. Each of the three stages refers to the relationship between the individual and their environment.

Personal signs are Aries, Taurus, Gemini, Cancer, and houses 1 through 4. Psychologically, they are considered premoral. Personal signs are generally focused on themselves and getting their immediate needs met. They are instinctual, independent, and self-motivated. If you lack this orientation, you may find it challenging to fulfill survival needs.

Social signs are Leo, Virgo, Libra, Scorpio, and houses 5 through 8. They are moral and have a strong desire to relate with others. Social signs are more interpersonal and concerned about their place in society and how others get along. They are social, compromising, and accepting. If you lack this orientation, you may find you lack social connection.

The Building Blocks of Astrology

Transpersonal signs are Sagittarius, Capricorn, Aquarius, Pisces, and houses 9 through 12. Transpersonal signs are most interested in their relationship with the universe. They are not concerned with personal or social morality, but rather with the highest ethics, regardless of who, what, or where. If you lack this orientation, you may find it challenging to connect with the world as a whole.

Your birth chart may have a dominant orientation, where most of your planets fall in one or two orientations. Knowing your dominant orientation can help you make sense of your approach to life and give you an understanding of how someone with a different orientation may have different values.

THE TEN PLANETS

Planets are the physical entities in the sky that we track in astrology. The planets in the birth chart represent an aspect of your personality and dimension of human experience. Each planet symbolizes something that rules over a different part of your psyche and is expressed differently in each sign and house.

There are a total of ten planets, divided into four different types: luminaries, inner planets, social planets, and outer planets.

The Sun and the Moon are luminaries. They are the most abundant sources of life on Earth and rule day and night. The Sun is our life force and self-expression, while the Moon is our inner world and emotional body.

The inner planets are physically closer to Earth and represent your psychological approach to interpersonal interactions. Mercury gives insight into your mental patterns, thought process, and communication. Venus indicates what you value and how you want to feel loved. Mars is the planet of action and represents your passion and drive.

The social planets are the most distant planets visible to the naked eye from Earth and represent themes related to society and collective consciousness. Jupiter is where you find luck and abundance. Saturn is the planet of structure and indicates your life lessons.

The outer planets are farthest from Earth and define larger life themes experienced by generations. Uranus is the planet of revolution and shows how you express your uniqueness. Neptune is your connection to spirituality. Pluto, considered a planet in the context of astrology, is the most powerful planet and represents transformation.

THE TWELVE HOUSES

The twelve houses represent areas of human life on Earth. They ground planets and signs into your lived experience. When an astrologer makes an interpretation or prediction, they use the houses to determine where in your life this energy will impact you.

There are several approaches to calculating houses depending on which house system is preferred. All house systems calculate divisions of the ecliptic plane.

Regardless of how an astrologer chooses to calculate houses, the first house begins with your rising sign and is known as the house of self, then each house expands outward into society and onward to your connection to the universe. The first six houses are personal houses and can be found below the horizon on the bottom half of the chart. The last six houses are interpersonal houses and can be found above the horizon on the top half of the chart.

The houses in your individual birth chart are determined based on the exact time and location of your birth. Your rising sign then determines which sign of the zodiac rules over every house in your chart. It is not possible to calculate your rising sign and therefore the rest of the houses in your chart without this information. If you do not have the time and location of your birth, some astrologers will do a chart rectification. The astrologer will compare important dates and events in your life with different potential birth charts to assume a likely time of birth.

Each of the twelve houses is discussed in detail in individual chapters in part II.

The Building Blocks of Astrology   **21**

THE POWER OF DISCOVERING YOUR UNIQUE HOROSCOPE

You may read your horoscope and wonder how astrologers depict something that resonates so much with you. Alternatively, you may read your horoscope and not relate to it at all. If your experience is the latter, let's talk about why.

Horoscopes are written for the twelve signs of the zodiac and therefore are often general. You likely read your horoscope for your zodiac sign or, as you now know it, your Sun sign. This is actually not how you should be reading horoscopes. Most horoscopes are written for your rising sign. Astrologers use your rising sign to determine which house or houses will be impacted by the current location of the planets. Therefore, the house, or area of life impacted, may or may not relate to the location of the Sun in your birth chart.

Therefore, understanding the building blocks of astrology is so important in helping empower you on your journey of personal growth. By understanding planets, signs, and houses, you can have insight into what is happening (planets), how it is happening (signs), and where it is happening (houses).

The planets, signs, and houses in your chart are unique to you based on your exact time and location of birth. You are the only person to experience them in this way. Understanding your unique birth chart can help you find validation in who you are and provide guidance in how to best nurture yourself and take action toward your future goals and desires.

KEY TAKEAWAYS

By breaking down the building blocks of astrology—the planets, signs, and houses—astrology can be accessible and easily applied to daily life. Understanding your unique birth chart can help you find validation in who you are and live an authentic life.

- There are twelve zodiac signs, which can be grouped by elements, polarities, modalities, or orientations. The signs speak to your unique qualities, behavioral style, and relationship between you and your environment.

- There are ten planets that represent an aspect of your personality and dimension of human experience. The four types are luminaries, inner planets, social planets, and outer planets.

- There are twelve houses that represent areas of human life on Earth. They ground planets and signs into your lived experience.

- Your unique birth chart consists of all twelve signs, twelve houses, and ten planets. The planets, signs, and houses in your chart are unique to you based on your exact time and location of birth. You are the only person to experience them in this way.

- Read the horoscope for your rising sign. Astrologers use your rising sign to determine which house will be impacted by the current location of the planets.

CHAPTER 3

THE BASICS OF
READING BIRTH CHARTS

Now that you understand the building blocks of astrology, it is time to dive into the essential information needed for reading and interpreting birth charts. In this chapter, you will learn what information is needed to pull a complete birth chart, the best websites for accessing your chart, and step-by-step instructions on how to interpret a birth chart. For this section, it is recommended you have both your birth chart and perhaps a friend or family member's birth chart to practice.

You will also learn other significant ways to look at a birth chart, including the angles, aspects, and stelliums and how the two wheels of astrology interact. Understanding houses, signs, and planets is essential for interpreting these components of a chart. Be sure to review chapter 2 if you need a refresher on the building blocks of astrology.

Once you learn the basics of reading your birth chart, you will understand how it can be such a powerful catalyst to meaningful growth. Your birth chart provides a complete understanding of your unique personality and potential life path. As you learn more about yourself through your birth chart, you will continue to peel back layers and have a deeper understanding of yourself.

SIGNIFICANCE OF A BIRTH CHART

Understanding your birth chart can be life-changing. It provides an illuminating and holistic understanding of your personality and potential life path. Your birth chart is a personal map to learn how to relate to others and yourself. It provides insight into all aspects of the human experience, such as how you process emotions, the most effective way for you to communicate, the way you love and want to feel loved, and what life lessons you need to experience to move toward your highest potential.

The birth chart is complex, but interpreting your chart does not need to be as hard as it looks. Though the full study of astrology can take a lifetime, there are a few areas that can be broken down to make astrology as simple as possible so that you can understand your own innate characteristics.

As you move through the rest of the workbook, you will need a copy of your birth chart accessible. There are several free websites and apps where you can easily input your birth information to get a copy of your birth chart. The website astro.com is one of the most easily accessible and informative. The app TimePassages is a simple app that also provides daily and long-term transit horoscopes.

The Date, Time, and Location of Your Birth

This is the most crucial piece of information you need in order to pull your birth chart. The date alone can give us an understanding of the sign most of the planets are in, but if any of the planets are changing signs that day, then your exact birth time is necessary. But the date does not give you information about the houses in your chart. The exact time and location (city and country) of your birth provide information on where your rising sign is and therefore where the houses fall in your chart and which zodiac signs rule that area of life in your chart.

Zodiac Signs

The signs in your birth chart represent how you are experiencing a certain area of your life. You have all twelve zodiac signs in your chart, but depending on planet placements and house rulers, some might be more emphasized than others.

Each zodiac sign will make up a 30-degree sector in your birth chart. They will always be in the same order, going counterclockwise around the wheel. What is unique to your birth chart is which sign begins your 1st house, also known as your rising sign. Your exact time and location of birth are needed for this.

Planets

The planets in your birth chart represent what you are experiencing in the corresponding parts of your life. Each of the planets in the birth chart represents an aspect of your personality and dimension of human experience. Each planet symbolizes something that rules over a different part of your psyche and is expressed differently in each sign and house.

There are a total of ten planets in every birth chart. Your birth chart is a snapshot of the sky at the moment of your birth, revealing the exact locations of the planets, as well as the signs of the zodiac they were in, at the time you entered the world.

Houses

The twelve houses represent where you are experiencing the what (planets) and the how (signs). They are areas of human life on Earth. The houses ground planets and signs into your unique lived experience.

The houses in your individual birth chart are determined based on the exact time and location of your birth. While the signs of the zodiac each make up 30 degrees in your chart, the houses will vary in size. Your time of birth indicates what sign was rising in the east at the moment of your birth, also known as your rising sign. Your rising sign then determines which sign of the zodiac rules over every house in your chart.

READING AND INTERPRETING YOUR BIRTH CHART

Once you have the date, time, and location of your birth, you can get started on diving into your birth chart. Since there are so many components to it, astrology can feel overwhelming, but by breaking it down into building blocks of astrology, you can make it feel much more approachable. Though a professional astrologer will best understand the nuances of your birth chart, you have the capability to

The Basics of Reading Birth Charts **27**

learn the basics of astrology well enough to begin the journey of self-growth and self-empowerment.

As mentioned previously, the website astro.com and the app TimePassages are two of the most easily accessible places to pull your birth chart from. You'll need this for the rest of the workbook. These websites will even provide you with some basic interpretations of your birth chart, but it is empowering to be able to read and interpret the chart yourself.

The key components of every chart are the planets, signs, and houses. If you understand these basics, you can get a clear picture of the overall chart, including the balance of the elements, modalities, and orientations in your chart. Once you have this foundation, you can also get into deeper components, such as the angles and aspects.

Follow the four simple steps on this page and the next to begin reading and interpreting your chart. Refer back to chapter 2 if you need support in identifying and interpreting each component. You may also find it helpful to have your friends', family members', or partner's charts available to begin practicing looking at different charts.

1. Where is each planet located in your chart?

    Make a table with ten rows and three columns. In the first column list all ten planets. In the second and third columns list the sign and house in which they are located in your chart, respectively. Most websites will provide a table indicating which zodiac sign each planet is in. You will likely need to look at the wheel to locate the house. You will see a number from 1 through 12 on the inner wheel, which represents the house. Under each planet, sign, and house in your table, list the qualities associated with each. You now have a visual representation of how each planet in your chart acts (sign) and where it occurs (house).

2. What zodiac sign rules each house in your chart?

    Each house will start with one sign and could end with either that same sign or a different sign. The sign that begins each house is the sign that rules that house in your birth chart. The qualities of this sign give insight into how you will experience that area of life, or house, regardless of what planets are or are not located there.

28   The Step-by-Step Astrology Workbook

Make a new table with two columns. List houses 1 through 12 in one column and the sign of the zodiac that begins each house in the second column. Under each sign and house, list the qualities associated with each to get an understanding of how you experience that part of your human experience.

3. Is there a balance of elements and modalities?

    Each of the three elements and four modalities is necessary for human life. Your birth chart may be balanced in all three elements and four modalities, or it may have a heavy focus in one or two. Most websites will provide a table that represents how many planets you have in each sign or modality. If they do not, you can use the list you created in instruction one to identify how many planets you have in each. This will give you an idea of your dominant elements and modalities and is the simplest way to get an overview of your chart.

4. Is there a stellium, or heavy concentration, in your chart?

    Look back at your table from step 1. Do you have multiple planets in one sign or house? If you have three or more planets in one sign or house, then you have a stellium in that sign or house. This means your life path has a focus here. Stelliums are discussed in depth on pages 31 and 32. If you do not have a stellium, then your birth chart is likely more spread out and has a balance of where the planets are located. Neither are right or wrong, but focused energy is an indicator of how certain qualities show up for you.

The Basics of Reading Birth Charts   **29**

THE MEANING BEHIND BIRTH CHART PATTERNS

You may notice certain patterns in many birth charts. Marc Edumund Jones identified seven chart patterns by observing the way the planets are grouped or spread out in your birth chart.

Bowl chart: All planets are located in one half of the chart. This person will be highly focused, but also needs to learn to integrate the empty space opposing their focus.

Bucket chart: All planets except one are located in one half of the chart. The one planet opposing the other planets is the handle of the bucket and is a planet that has a strong influence on the individual.

Bundle chart: All planets are within four signs of the zodiac, creating several conjunctions and stelliums. There is likely a hyper focus in one or a few areas of life or a specialized area of expertise.

Locomotive chart: The planets are in eight continuous signs or houses, though one empty sign or house is allowed. This person's life is driven by the planet following the empty space.

Seesaw chart: The planets are grouped together in two clusters, opposite each other. A person with this pattern constantly feels like they are being pulled in two directions, trying to find balance.

Splash chart: Planets are not in a pattern. This person will have many interests but may lack focus.

Splay chart: The planets form at least two pairs of conjunctions and have at least one empty sign between them. A person with this pattern likely has strong interests or strengths in multiple areas.

ANGLES, ASCENDANTS, AND ASPECTS

Angles and aspects are crucial when going deeper into your birth chart. Angles are the two lines that divide your chart in half vertically and horizontally. Aspects are the lines that you see in the middle of your birth chart wheel.

The ascendent (AC), also known as your rising, and descendant (DC) divide the chart horizontally. The ascendant always begins your 1st house of self and indicates the lens you see the world through. The descendant begins your 7th house of others and provides insight into the kind of people you are attracted to in partnership. The midheaven (MC) and imum coeli (IC) divide the chart vertically. The midheaven always begins your 10th house of public life and career and identifies how the world will recognize your accomplishments. The imum coeli begins your 4th house of inner world and home and represents the least conscious part of yourself.

Aspects represent the way that the planets in your chart communicate with one another. Some are more harmonious, whereas others can feel more challenging. There are four main aspects. A conjunction is when two planets are within a few degrees of one another, typically in the same sign. A trine is when two planets are about 120 degrees apart, typically in the same element. A square is when two planets are about 90 degrees apart, typically in the same modality. An opposition is when two planets are about 180 degrees apart, typically in the same polarity.

UNDERSTANDING STELLIUMS

A stellium is when three or more planets are located in the same sign or the same house. If you have just two planets in the same sign or house, that is not considered a stellium; rather, it is a conjunction, which is much more common.

If you have a stellium, you will feel the energy of that sign or house deeply throughout your life. If the stellium consists of mostly personal planets, then you may notice it more regularly in your daily life. For example, if you have a stellium in the 10th house, you may feel validated in how career driven you are. If the stellium is made up of mostly outer planets, it may be more difficult to notice from day to day, but it will have a big impact on your life path.

The Basics of Reading Birth Charts   **31**

It is important to dive deeper into the meanings of each of the planets involved. If it is a stellium involving the Sun (identity), Moon (emotions), and Venus (love), that is going to be a much different focus then if it were Saturn (lessons), Uranus (rebellion), and Pluto (transformation).

The sign or house that your stellium is located in can be a gift because you have such strength in that area of your chart. However, this can also be draining if you do not have any planets in the opposite sign to balance the energy. You may feel as though there is too much emphasis in one area of your life, and it may require a more conscious effort to activate the other areas of your chart.

THE RELATIONSHIP BETWEEN THE TWO WHEELS OF ASTROLOGY

An astrological chart is divided into twelve sectors, two different ways. The outer wheel is the zodiac, with each sign making up 30 degrees of the wheel. The inner wheel is the houses, varying in size, but still totaling 360 degrees of the wheel. The circle in the middle of the wheel represents Earth.

The outer wheel consists of all twelve signs of the zodiac in the same order, moving counterclockwise around the wheel. Though we know the planets actually orbit around the Sun, the wheel represents how each planet passes through the signs from our viewpoint on Earth. Any planets above Earth on the wheel are transiting above Earth's horizon and could theoretically be seen at the time of your birth; any planets below Earth in the wheel are transiting below the horizon. Where in the wheel each sign is located in your chart is determined by your rising sign. For example, if you are a Libra rising, Libra will start your 1st house, and its polarity, Aries, will start your 7th house directly opposite.

The inner wheel consists of all twelve houses in the same order, in the same location in the chart, moving counterclockwise around the wheel. The 1st house will always start at nine o'clock, or on the left of the wheel in the middle, which is the point of the ecliptic that was on the eastern horizon at the moment of your birth. The 7th house will always be directly opposite, starting at three o'clock, or on the right of the wheel in the middle, representing the western horizon.

What It Means to Have Empty Houses

It is likely that one or more of the houses in your chart does not have any planets located in it. This is considered an empty house. It does not mean that this area of your life is empty or does not exist. It just means there are not planets, or actors, there actively playing it out on a daily basis. To learn more about how this area shows up in your life, you can look at what sign begins that house. This is the ruling sign of that house and gives you an idea of the flavor that shows up here for you.

The Power of Free Will

Though astrology can provide guidance, insight, and a suggested path forward, you have free will. This is what makes you human. In every action you take, it is your decision how you exercise your power. By understanding your chart, you can feel validated in choices you've made or perhaps have clarity on where you've chosen a more challenging path. Under no circumstances should astrology be used as a crutch or as an excuse to be or not to be a certain way. Rather, it should be used as an empowerment tool that makes you aware of all your options.

APPLYING YOUR BIRTH CHART'S FINDINGS TO YOUR LIFE

Understanding your birth chart can be a catalyst to meaningful growth. It provides a complete understanding of your unique personality and potential life path. As you learn more about yourself through your birth chart, you will continue to peel back layers and have a deeper understanding of yourself.

Your birth chart provides insight into all aspects of the human experience. Learning how to meaningfully read and interpret a birth chart can support you in understanding not only how you process emotions, how you communicate, the way you love, and what you value, but also how these things show up in each area of your life. For example, the way you process emotions may look different in your dynamic with your parents than it does in your dynamic with your romantic partner or in a business setting.

The Basics of Reading Birth Charts   **33**

Knowing that you have a unique birth chart identifying these qualities in you, you may also find that you have more compassion toward others, as their birth charts are unique in their own right. Other people are going to experience emotions differently than you and communicate those in a way that makes sense perhaps only to them. Understanding that every person operates in a unique way allows you to have appreciation for differences instead of fighting against them.

Your chart also shows where your deep-rooted fears, core beliefs, and perhaps limiting beliefs come from.

These are all part of the life lessons that you need to experience in order to move toward your highest potential, and they also reveal what your highest life path looks like.

KEY TAKEAWAYS

Understanding the basics of reading a birth chart shows you what a powerful tool astrology is for meaningful growth. Your birth chart provides a holistic understanding of your innate characteristics and potential life path across all aspects of human experience.

- ◆ You need your birth time, date, and location (city and country) to get a copy of your birth chart or someone else's birth chart. Plug this information into astro.com or the TimePassages app.

- ◆ The first step of interpreting your birth chart includes identifying the location of each of the planets, including what sign and house it is located in.

- ◆ After identifying the location of each planet, you can look at overall themes, such as the balance of elements or modalities, and determine whether there is a heavy concentration of planets in one or more areas of your birth chart.

- ◆ Though astrology can provide deep insight into your character and potential future, you have free will. This is what makes you human. Astrology should not be used as an excuse or crutch; rather, it should empower you.

- ◆ Understanding your uniqueness through your birth chart allows you to have appreciation not only for yourself but also for differences in others.

PART II

YOUR BIRTH CHART AND THE TWELVE HOUSES OF ASTROLOGY IN ACTION

You've learned in the first part of this book that the twelve houses represent areas of human life on Earth, grounding the planets and signs into your lived experiences. In this part, you will discover what each house represents in your birth chart, through twelve chapters that are each individually dedicated to diving deep into a particular house. You will need a copy of your birth chart to move through each exercise. It is important that you have the correct time and location of birth, as this is how the houses are determined.

There are related exercises in each chapter that will better inform your understanding of the houses in your birth chart. The way that the houses are laid out in your chart is one of the reasons your chart is so unique to you, as everyone will have different house rulers and planetary placements within each house.

As you move through the exercises in the first six houses, you may notice that these topics are more personal, whereas the latter six houses are more interpersonal and represent relational areas of life. By the end of each chapter you will have a more comprehensive and individualized understanding of your personality and how you experience certain areas of life.

CHAPTER 4

THE 1ST HOUSE
OF ASTROLOGY

THE HOUSE OF SELF

In order to understand yourself at a foundational level, it is important to start by unpacking your identity, which can be found in the 1st house. This is also crucial in understanding the rest of your chart, as it represents the lens you see the world through and therefore the lens you see the rest of your chart through.

In this chapter, you will learn about the Aries-ruled 1st house and how it governs the conscious self, your identity, and how you are seen by others. Using your birth chart, you will then move through five workbook exercises designed to help you navigate interpreting your chart through the 1st astrological house.

While you can study the general themes of the 1st house and have a good understanding of its meaning, because houses ground your lived experiences, only you can know exactly how this particular area of life shows up for you. The workbook exercises help focus you on the themes of self, identity, and consciousness so that you can have a more precise understanding of how you currently experience your 1st house and also where you have room to grow.

THE INFLUENCE OF THE 1ST HOUSE

The 1st house is ruled by Aries and represents the conscious self, your identity, and how you are seen by others. This is the initial house and therefore where everything begins, where seeds are planted, and where life is initiated. It is all about the identification of self and the realization of your ultimate potential.

The rising sign, or ascendant, is always located in the 1st house. This makes this area of the chart especially important because not only is this a major indicator of your identity, but it also determines how the rest of the houses are placed in your birth chart. Any planets in your birth chart located in the 1st house will have a strong effect on your personality and identity.

The 1st house also represents your physical body and appearance. As the first area of life in your chart, it is how you came into this world at birth, also understood as how you entered your physical body. It can be an indicator of your actual physical appearance and also your first impression of and how you understand the world around you.

As the Aries-ruled house, it also holds your warrior energy. It is where you may find your courage, your chi energy, and your motivations. It demands self-reflection, because it is also where you have the most room for continued self-improvement. Since the 1st house represents your first breath on Earth, it shapes your entire life, but more importantly, it speaks to how you develop throughout your life as you uncover your highest potential.

YOUR BIRTH CHART

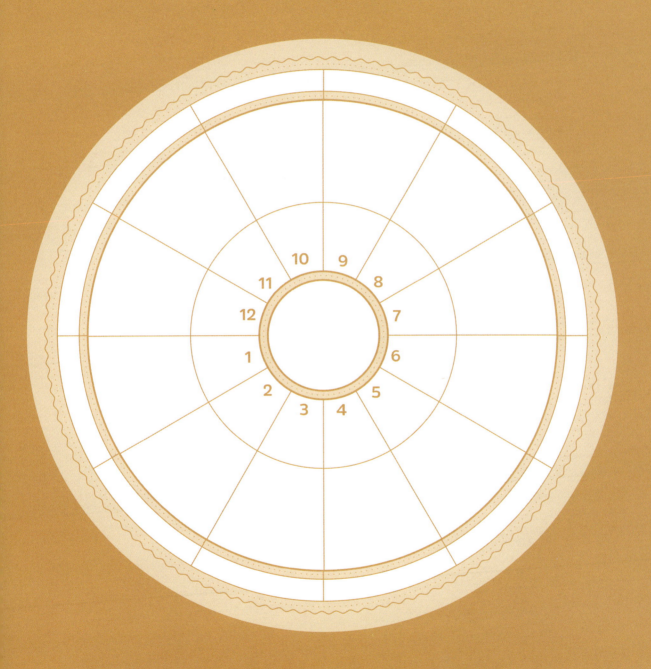

⭕ EXERCISE 1

While Aries typically rules the 1st house, your chart will show a unique sign here. More than one sign is possible. The 1st house ruling sign is at the start of the house, close to the 12th and farthest from the 2nd.

Fill in the four blanks at the end of this exercise by following these steps:

1. Find the sign that rules your 1st house in your birth chart. This starts the house.

2. Find the planet that rules this sign in the following table. Look for the planet in your chart to discover its house.

3. Determine the meaning of the house that holds your 1st house ruling planet.

The 1st house in my chart is ruled by _____ (sign). The sign that rules my 1st house is ruled by _____ (planet). The planet that rules my 1st house is in the _____ (house). This house represents _____ (house meaning). Since my conscious self shows up here, I have the greatest potential for deepening my sense of identity.

SIGN	RULING PLANET		HOUSE	HOUSE MEANING
Aries	Mars		1	Self, identity, physical body
Taurus	Venus		2	Values, money, resources
Gemini	Mercury		3	Intellect, communication, community
Cancer	Moon		4	Subconscious, psychologist, home
Leo	Sun		5	Creativity, children, love, play
Virgo	Mercury		6	Service, health, details, work
Libra	Venus		7	Relationships, harmony, balance
Scorpio	Pluto		8	Underworld, therapists, depth
Sagittarius	Jupiter		9	Higher education, philosophy, travel
Capricorn	Saturn		10	Ambition, reputation, career
Aquarius	Uranus		11	Technology, friends, innovation
Pisces	Neptune		12	Psychic, secrets, boundaries, past lives

42   *The Step-by-Step Astrology Workbook*

EXERCISE 2

This exercise will help you understand how your 1st house is influenced by your birth chart placements. In the first column of the following table, circle your 1st house planets. Then read the correlating descriptions in the second column to see how you experience each planet.

1ST HOUSE PLANETS	1ST HOUSE EXPERIENCES
No planets in the 1st house	Review exercise 1 to learn which planet rules your 1st house. Find that planet in your birth chart. The sign that holds this planet will help you understand your 1st house.
Sun	Your identity shines through in the way you express yourself. You have a strong sense of identity.
Moon	You wear your emotional body on your sleeve. You need to feel free to express your ever-changing moods.
Mercury	You lead with your intellect and are naturally curious.
Venus	You value taking initiative and you radiate beauty.
Mars	You need to release energy through movement and appear confident.
Jupiter	You are larger than life and appear open-minded.
Saturn	You are responsible and a hard worker but are still learning how to assert yourself.
Uranus	You don't like to follow rules and prefer to stand out.
Neptune	You intuitively know who you are and can feel your environment energetically.
Pluto	You have strong personal power, and people are drawn to you.

The 1st House of Astrology   43

☾ EXERCISE 3

The Aries-ruled 1st house represents your identity and is where you find your chi energy. The goal is to feel empowered by your identity and have no fear in being exactly who you are. This takes courage, some risk-taking, and self-assertion. Since it is the 1st house, it is also the beginning of anything you do or create. This is how you start new projects and where you create anything new. Use the journal prompts that follow to reflect on the themes of the 1st house.

1. What is courage? What does it mean to you?

2. Think about a time when acting courageously failed you or hurt you. What happened? If you could, would you do anything differently?

3. What is risk? What does it mean to you?

4. Think about a time when taking a risk failed or hurt you. What happened? If you could, would you do anything differently?

5. What is anger? What does it mean to you?

6. Think about a time when acting out of anger failed or hurt you. What happened? If you could, would you do anything differently?

7. Is there part of you that you are still hiding from others, or even hiding from yourself?

8. Where are you still limiting yourself? Where does this limiting belief come from?

9. What is something you want to start? What is holding you back?

10. What "I am" statements can you affirm to yourself daily, bringing you back to your own power? (Examples: *I am powerful. I am worthy. I am abundant. I am successful.*)

EXERCISE 4

In this exercise, you will learn the meaning of the placement of your 1st house ruler. In the following chart, identify your 1st house ruler and read the interpretation. For example, if your 1st house is ruled by Capricorn, then your 1st house ruler is Saturn, so look to see where Saturn is in your chart. If you see Saturn is in your 4th house, read the 4th house interpretation. Fill in the blanks:

My 1st house ruler is in the _____ (house). This means that my conscious self directs my life's motivations in the direction of _____ _____.

RULER OF THE 1ST HOUSE IS IN YOUR . . .	MY CONSCIOUS SELF DIRECTS MY LIFE'S MOTIVATIONS IN THE DIRECTION OF . . .
1st house	my own priorities and self-development.
2nd house	my financial security and self-worth.
3rd house	my local community, and communication.
4th house	my home, legacy, and traditions.
5th house	my self-expression and creative work.
6th house	my service to others and personal health.
7th house	collaboration and relationship to others.
8th house	understanding people, no matter how dark.
9th house	understanding philosophies, cultures, and belief systems.
10th house	making a known impact on the world.
11th house	creating community and humanitarian efforts.
12th house	understanding something greater than myself.

The 1st House of Astrology

EXERCISE 5

Respond to the statements in the following self-care checklist to discover whether you are in touch with the themes of the 1st house. If you answer mostly true, you likely already feel empowered in this area of your life. If you answer mostly false, it is nothing to stress about. It simply means you need to focus on this area of life more. It would also be helpful to lean into the qualities of the zodiac sign that is in this area of your chart. The journal prompts in exercise 3 on page 44 and this self-care checklist can support you in your journey of unpacking the themes of this house.

I have a clear sense of identity.	True	Sometimes True	Sometimes False	False
I live my life from a place of courage. Nothing scares me.	True	Sometimes True	Sometimes False	False
As long as they are aligned with my authenticity, I like to take risks.	True	Sometimes True	Sometimes False	False
I am able to feel, process, and express my anger in a healthy way.	True	Sometimes True	Sometimes False	False
I don't hide any part of myself. I feel free to be me.	True	Sometimes True	Sometimes False	False
When I have an idea, I take action to get it started.	True	Sometimes True	Sometimes False	False
I know what I want and so do others, because I don't keep anything hidden.	True	Sometimes True	Sometimes False	False
I know how to confidently and eloquently assert myself, even if it is a sensitive subject.	True	Sometimes True	Sometimes False	False

46   The Step-by-Step Astrology Workbook

KEY TAKEAWAYS

The 1st house of identity is the first area of life in your birth chart, and understanding and unpacking how you experience it is a crucial foundation for understanding the rest of your chart.

- Your rising sign, or ascendent, is always in the 1st house. The sign of your rising sign determines how the rest of your houses are placed in your birth chart and what signs rule each house.

- The planets represent an aspect of your personality. Any planets located in the 1st house influence your identity and provide an additional layer of how you experience your motivations in life, others' first impressions of you, and your physical body.

- An individual's relationship with their identity is complex and unique to them. Taking time to journal on the themes of the 1st house, such as courage, risk, anger, and limiting beliefs, can help empower you to live as a more authentic version of who you already are.

- Understanding the house placement of your 1st house ruler provides a deeper insight into your conscious self and life's motivations.

- Saying or writing "I am" affirmation statements daily will help bring you back to your power.

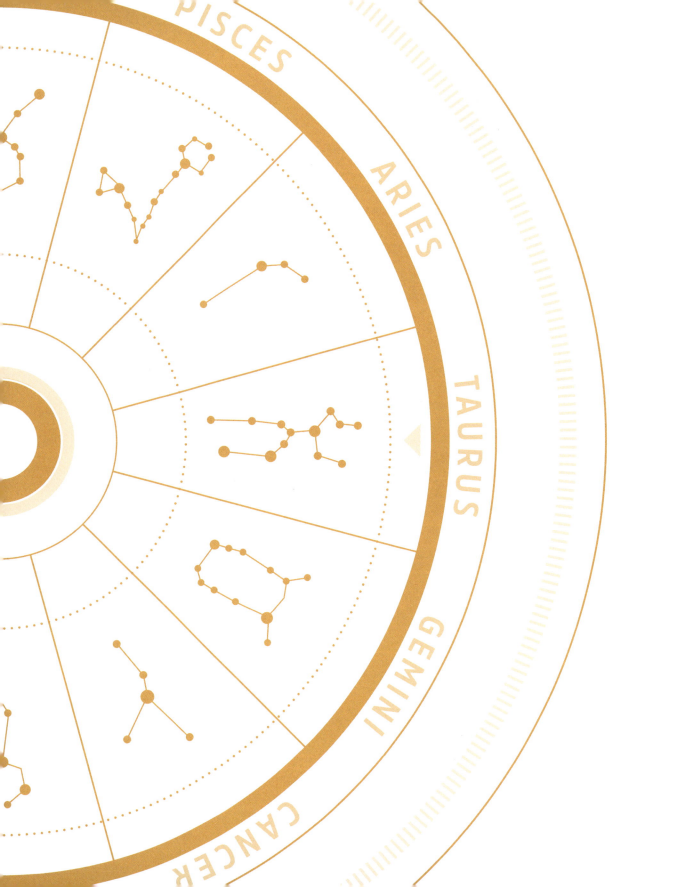

CHAPTER 5

THE 2ND HOUSE OF ASTROLOGY

THE HOUSE OF VALUE

In order to understand your value system, it is important to start by unpacking your relationship with self-worth, which can be found in the 2nd house. This also supports you in understanding the rest of your chart, as living true to your value system is the foundation to how you consciously operate in the other areas of your life.

In this chapter, you will learn about the Taurus-ruled 2nd house and how it governs the material world and financial standing. Using your birth chart, you will then move through five workbook exercises designed to help you navigate interpreting your chart through the 2nd astrological house.

While you can study the general themes of the 2nd house and have a good understanding of its meaning, because houses ground your lived experiences, only you can know exactly how this particular area of life shows up for you. The workbook exercises help focus you on the themes of values, self-worth, and money so that you can have a more precise understanding of how you currently experience your 2nd house and also where you have room to let go of limiting beliefs and live a life of abundance.

THE INFLUENCE OF THE 2ND HOUSE

The 2nd house is ruled by Taurus and represents resources, finances, the material world, all earthbound things, and the five senses. It also indicates what you value in life and your relationship with self-worth. This is the area of your chart where you can understand what makes you feel stable and secure, especially in relation to money and resources.

The 2nd house is the ruler of the five physical senses, and if you have planets in it, you likely enjoy experiencing life through all things beautiful and simple—good-smelling candles, cozy blankets, calm ambience. This house is motivated by understanding the true value and worth of material things, whether they cost a lot of money or not. As long as the things make you feel secure and are pleasing to the five senses, the 2nd house reminds us that they are valuable.

The 2nd house rules our personal finances and relationship with money or feelings toward financial assets. It may indicate that you are more likely to have a large savings account and never spend it—or, alternatively, that you overspend. Both of these actions are triggered by feelings around security. The former may be because you have had things taken from you and you overcompensate by excess saving, whereas the latter may be because you find your sense of worth through material goods.

The power of the 2nd house is to show you what makes you feel worthy and valued. Living in alignment with your values will inherently support you in feeling worthy from within.

YOUR BIRTH CHART

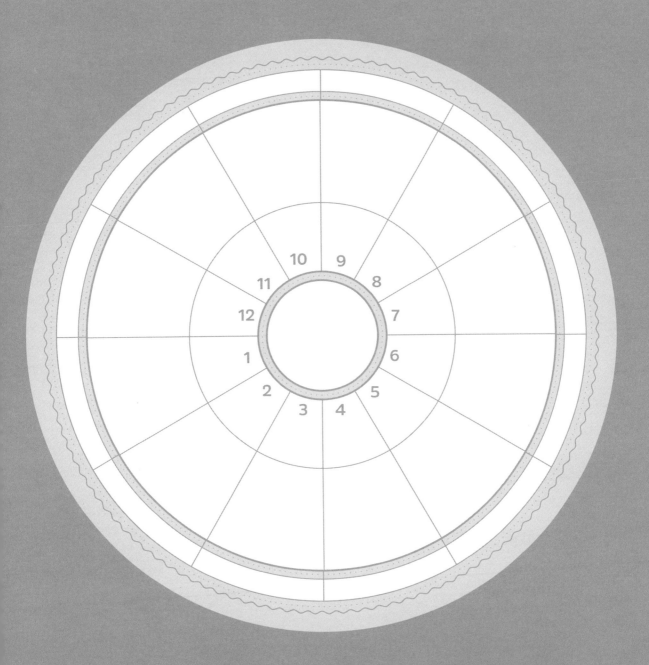

◯ EXERCISE 1

Although the 2nd house is naturally ruled by Taurus, your personal birth chart will have a unique zodiac sign flavoring the energy of your 2nd house. There may be one or more signs that take up space in your 2nd house. The sign that is considered the ruler of your 2nd house will be at the beginning of the house, closest to the 1st house and farthest from the 3rd.

Fill in the four blanks at the end of this exercise by following these steps:

1. Review your birth chart to see what sign rules your 2nd house. This is the sign that starts the house.

2. Use the table on page 42 to see what planet rules that particular sign. This is your 2nd house ruling planet. Find that planet in your chart to see in which house it is located.

3. Use the table to determine the meaning of the house that holds your 2nd house ruling planet.

The 2nd house in my birth chart is ruled by _____ (sign). The sign that rules my 2nd house is ruled by _____ (planet). The planet that rules my personal 2nd house is located in the _____ (house) in my birth chart. This house represents _____ (house meaning). My values also show up in this area of life. Since what I value shows up in this area of life, I also have the greatest potential for living in alignment with what I care most about.

52   The Step-by-Step Astrology Workbook

☾ EXERCISE 2

This exercise will help you understand how your 2nd house is influenced by your birth chart placements. In the first column of the following table, circle your 2nd house planets. Then read the correlating descriptions in the second column to see how you experience each planet.

2ND HOUSE PLANETS	2ND HOUSE EXPERIENCES
No planets in the 2nd house	Review exercise 1 to learn which planet rules your 2nd house. Find that planet in your birth chart. The sign that holds this planet will help you understand your 2nd house.
Sun	You are grounded in your identity and feel secure in expressing yourself.
Moon	You seek emotional stability and groundedness. You are dependent on others' feedback or your personal belongings to feel worthy.
Mercury	You have a logical mind and are likely good with numbers.
Venus	You need tangible expressions of love and value the simple things.
Mars	You seek security and release energy through working hard.
Jupiter	You have faith that you will receive enough income to feel secure.
Saturn	You have lessons to learn around finances and resources, but if you learn from your lessons, they will quite literally pay off.
Uranus	You likely earn money in a unique way or have fluctuations in your income.
Neptune	You have the ability to make money through the arts or spirituality.
Pluto	You feel a need to have control over your finances and may be possessive over your material items.

The 2nd House of Astrology   **53**

EXERCISE 3

The Taurus-ruled 2nd house represents your values, self-worth, and relationship with money. According to the 2nd house, these are all inextricably connected. Getting clear on your values and confident in your self-worth from the inside out can support your relationship with money. Your relationship with money also stems from your childhood and how people around you today speak about money. Use the journal prompts that follow to reflect on the themes of the 2nd house.

1. Is abundance hard to obtain? Why or why not?

2. What makes you feel stable and secure?

3. Do you feel inner peace? When do you feel the most peaceful? How can you restore your inner peace?

4. Do you have access to nature? What is your relationship with the natural world around you? How can you explore nature using your five senses?

5. How do you talk about money? Are you a spender, saver, or avoider? How did your parents talk about money? How do people in your life talk about money? Are they spenders, savers, or avoiders?

6. What values do you consider most important? How do your actions align with those values?

7. What makes you feel worthy?

8. Do you tie your sense of worth to how much money you make or have? Why or why not?

9. What does financial freedom mean to you?

10. Write about your future self in the present tense. What is your life like? What resources do you have? In what ways are you feeling fulfilled? How do you define your worth and how do you feel about that?

54   The Step-by-Step Astrology Workbook

EXERCISE 4

In this exercise, you will learn the meaning of the placement of your 2nd house ruler. In the following chart, identify your 2nd house ruler and read the interpretation. For example, if your 2nd house is ruled by Aquarius, then your 2nd house ruler is Uranus, so look to see where Uranus is in your chart. If you see Uranus is in your 4th house, read the 4th house interpretation. Fill in the blanks:

My 2nd house ruler is in the _____ (house). This means that my resources, income, and self-worth are _____ _____.

RULER OF THE 2ND HOUSE IS IN YOUR...	MY RESOURCES, INCOME, AND SELF-WORTH ARE...
1st house	in my own hands. I am in control.
2nd house	increased by how I manage what I already have.
3rd house	from my local community and activated through communication.
4th house	related to my upbringing and my relationship with my parents.
5th house	connected to my creative pursuits and how I enjoy myself.
6th house	worked for through discipline and organization.
7th house	found in relationships or through contracts.
8th house	connected to other people, perhaps through inheritances.
9th house	found through searching for them, perhaps by traveling or studying.
10th house	driving my goals. I want to lead.
11th house	related to my network. I like to give and receive.
12th house	found through saving or more hidden matters.

The 2nd House of Astrology

EXERCISE 5

Respond to the statements in the following self-care checklist to discover whether you are in touch with the themes of the 2nd house. If you answer mostly true, you likely already feel empowered in this area of your life. If you answer mostly false, it is nothing to stress about. It simply means you need to focus on this area of life more. It would also be helpful to lean into the qualities of the zodiac sign that is in this area of your chart. The journal prompts in exercise 3 on page 54 and this self-care checklist can support you in your journey of unpacking the themes of this house.

I am clear on my values and live my life in alignment with them.	True	Sometimes True	Sometimes False	False
I know what makes me feel stable and secure.	True	Sometimes True	Sometimes False	False
I spend time in nature and activating my five senses.	True	Sometimes True	Sometimes False	False
Even without resources or money, I know I am worthy.	True	Sometimes True	Sometimes False	False
I spend time every day cultivating my inner worth.	True	Sometimes True	Sometimes False	False
I have a good relationship with money and do not have any fear around not having enough.	True	Sometimes True	Sometimes False	False
I know abundance is always possible.	True	Sometimes True	Sometimes False	False
I indulge in things that make me feel good. This shows my body and soul that I care about my worth.	True	Sometimes True	Sometimes False	False

56   The Step-by-Step Astrology Workbook

KEY TAKEAWAYS

Understanding and unpacking how you experience the 2nd house of values and resources can help you have a deeper sense of what it means to feel stable and secure, especially in terms of the material world.

- ◆ The 2nd house represents how you interact with the physical world through spending or saving money, obtaining material resources, and experiencing the five senses. Understanding this part of your chart can give you insight into your own self-worth.

- ◆ The planets represent an aspect of your personality. Any planets located in the 2nd house influence your values and provide an additional layer of how you experience abundance, resources, and material security.

- ◆ An individual's relationship with their self-worth is complex and unique to them. Taking time to journal on the themes of the 2nd house, such as stability, security, abundance, and money, can help empower you to live a life truly aligned with your values.

- ◆ Understanding the house placement of your 2nd house ruler provides a deeper insight into your resources, income, and self-worth.

- ◆ Journaling about your future self to identify what material resources and income you ideally want to have in your life can help bring this abundance into your life now.

The 2nd House of Astrology

CHAPTER 6

THE 3RD HOUSE OF ASTROLOGY

THE HOUSE OF COMMUNICATION

In order to understand your communication, it is important to start by unpacking your mind and how you process information, which can be found in the 3rd house. This is also a key component in understanding the rest of your chart, as it represents the way you connect with others, which is foundational in many areas of the human experience.

In this chapter, you will learn about the Gemini-ruled 3rd house and how it governs communications, correspondences, your intellect, and your social life. Using your birth chart, you will then move through five workbook exercises designed to help you navigate interpreting your chart through the 3rd astrological house.

While you can study the general themes of the 3rd house and have a good understanding of its meaning, because houses ground your lived experiences, only you can know exactly how this particular area of life shows up for you. The workbook exercises help focus you on the themes of education, communication, and your relationship with the local community, so that you can have a more precise understanding of how you currently experience your 3rd house and also where you have room to deepen your relationship to your mind and to others.

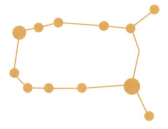

THE INFLUENCE OF THE 3RD HOUSE

The 3rd house is ruled by Gemini and represents communication, local community, and how you process information. It is where you can learn more about your early education, social interests, networking, and community events. The 3rd house is also the area of the chart that represents extended family, such as siblings, cousins, aunts, and uncles. It is a very active part of the chart, especially for the mind.

If you have planets in the 3rd house, it is likely that communication is a big theme in your life. You may be a good writer or speaker or simply have a need to express yourself through words. People with a lot of energy in this area of the chart also tend to be good multitaskers, but they may also seem scattered or unfocused because they are moving from one thought or topic to another so quickly. This is also why you may find that it is sometimes difficult to follow through on a task or commitment in this area of your life.

The 3rd house emphasizes connection. It is how you are connected to the people around you in your neighborhood and your family, and it can even represent social media. Feeling connected requires communication. Understanding this part of your chart can assist you in effectively communicating, which will support you in nurturing your connections.

The keys to your abilities to think, process, and share are all found in your 3rd house. You likely seek answers through this area of your chart and will often get them because you have endless curiosity through this lens.

YOUR BIRTH CHART

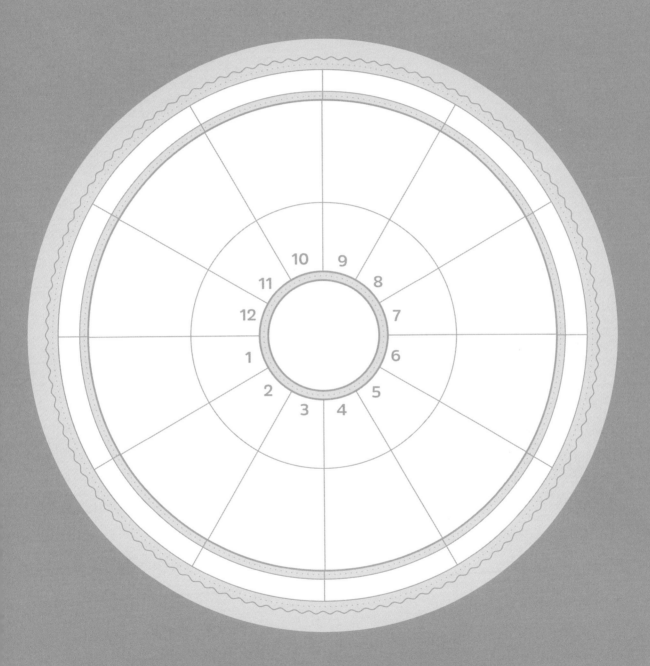

◯ EXERCISE 1

Although the 3rd house is naturally ruled by Gemini, your personal birth chart will have a unique zodiac sign flavoring the energy of your 3rd house. There may be one or more signs that take up space in your 3rd house. The sign that is considered the ruler of your 3rd house will be at the beginning of the house, closest to the 2nd house and farthest from the 4th.

Fill in the four blanks at the end of this exercise by following these steps:

1. Review your birth chart to see what sign rules your 3rd house. This is the sign that starts the house.

2. Use the table on page 42 to see what planet rules that particular sign. This is your 3rd house ruling planet. Find that planet in your chart to see in which house it is located.

3. Use the table to determine the meaning of the house that holds your 3rd house ruling planet.

The 3rd house in my birth chart is ruled by _____ (sign). The sign that rules my 3rd house is ruled by _____ (planet). The planet that rules my personal 3rd house is located in the _____ (house) in my birth chart. This house represents _____ (house meaning). The way I process information also shows up in this area of life. Since my mind shows up in this area of life, I also have the greatest potential for learning how to best express myself and feel understood.

62   The Step-by-Step Astrology Workbook

☾ EXERCISE 2

This exercise will help you understand how your 3rd house is influenced by your birth chart placements. In the first column of the following table, circle your 3rd house planets. Then read the correlating descriptions in the second column to see how you experience each planet.

3RD HOUSE PLANETS	3RD HOUSE EXPERIENCES
No planets in the 3rd house	Review exercise 1 to learn which planet rules your 3rd house. Find that planet in your birth chart. The sign that holds this planet will help you understand your 3rd house.
Sun	You are able to express yourself through connecting with others. You are a natural connector.
Moon	You need to be able to write or speak about your emotions. It is important to also feel and not just intellectualize your emotions.
Mercury	You are particularly curious and have a quick mind.
Venus	You need to connect intellectually, and you value people's words.
Mars	You release energy through connecting with your community.
Jupiter	You are a lifelong learner and constantly expand your knowledge.
Saturn	You have a desire to master a particular topic or field but are still learning how to communicate effectively.
Uranus	You are likely interested in many topics, especially more unique or progressive ideas.
Neptune	You are intuitive and poetic in the way you speak.
Pluto	You are passionate about a particular topic, possibly in the areas of psychology or investigative work, and will become an expert on it.

The 3rd House of Astrology   63

EXERCISE 3

The Gemini-ruled 3rd house represents communication, your mind and intellect, and local community. Use the journal prompts that follow to reflect on the themes of the 3rd house.

1. What does good communication look like to you? Are you actively practicing this yourself?

2. Do you silence part of yourself or feel afraid to communicate about certain topics? How does that make you feel?

3. If you could talk about anything for one hour, what would it be?

4. What area do you constantly research or want to learn more about? Are you someone who likes to learn a little bit about a lot of things, or do you want to master one topic?

5. Think about a time when you felt misunderstood or not heard. What happened? How did you feel? If you could, would you do anything differently?

6. Do you feel connected to your community or a group of friends?

7. Think about a time when you felt disconnected from those around you. What happened? How did you feel? If you could, would you do anything differently?

8. How do you process information? Do you always have the opportunity to process information in the way that works best for you?

9. Think about a time when you weren't given the opportunity to process information in the way that works best for you, perhaps in school or when training for a job. How did that make you feel?

10. What "I know" statements can you affirm to yourself daily, bringing you back to your personal intellectual power? (Examples: *I know I am prosperous. I know I am generous. I know I am powerful.*)

64   The Step-by-Step Astrology Workbook

EXERCISE 4

In this exercise, you will learn the meaning of the placement of your 3rd house ruler. In the following chart, identify your 3rd house ruler and read the interpretation. For example, if your 3rd house is ruled by Cancer, then your 3rd house ruler is the Moon, so look to see where the Moon is in your chart. If you see the Moon is in your 4th house, read the 4th house interpretation. Fill in the blanks:

My 3rd house ruler is in the _____ (house). This means that my community and communication priorities are _____
_____.

RULER OF THE 3RD HOUSE IS IN YOUR...	MY COMMUNITY AND COMMUNICATION PRIORITIES ARE...
1st house	my independence and expressing my identity.
2nd house	material resources, financial security, and expressing my values.
3rd house	the identity and structure of the local community.
4th house	my familial or ancestral roots and legacy.
5th house	my creativity, self-expression, and desire for pleasure.
6th house	my physical health, daily routines, and how I am of service to the community.
7th house	individual and contractual relationships.
8th house	unavoidable or hidden matters, such as death and taxes.
9th house	lifelong learning and seeking truth.
10th house	achievement and public perception.
11th house	to support the community through humanitarian efforts.
12th house	understanding secrets and establishing boundaries.

The 3rd House of Astrology

EXERCISE 5

Respond to the statements in the following self-care checklist to discover whether you are in touch with the themes of the 3rd house. If you answer mostly true, you likely already feel empowered in this area of your life. If you answer mostly false, it is nothing to stress about. It simply means you need to focus on this area of life more. It would also be helpful to lean into the qualities of the zodiac sign that is in this area of your chart. The journal prompts in exercise 3 on page 64 and this self-care checklist can support you in your journey of unpacking the themes of this house.

I practice active listening and am told by others that I am a good listener.	True	Sometimes True	Sometimes False	False
I feel confident in communicating my needs.	True	Sometimes True	Sometimes False	False
I know the way my mind works is unique to me, and I make sure that I have the resources needed to learn best.	True	Sometimes True	Sometimes False	False
I ask questions when I don't understand something.	True	Sometimes True	Sometimes False	False
I feel connected to my community.	True	Sometimes True	Sometimes False	False
When my interests change, I am not afraid to change course and focus on something new.	True	Sometimes True	Sometimes False	False
I am a lifelong learner. Even when I've mastered something, there is always more to learn.	True	Sometimes True	Sometimes False	False
I am not afraid to have difficult conversations.	True	Sometimes True	Sometimes False	False

66   The Step-by-Step Astrology Workbook

KEY TAKEAWAYS

Understanding and unpacking how you experience the 3rd house of your mind, local community, and how you process information can support you in effectively communicating and nurturing connections.

◆ The 3rd house represents your early education, social interests, and local community. It is the foundation of how you express yourself through words and process what others share with you through their words.

◆ The planets represent an aspect of your personality. Any planets located in the 3rd house influence your communication style and provide an additional layer of how you listen to others, your connection to your community and your interests, and your ease in expanding your knowledge.

◆ An individual's mind is complex and unique to them. Taking time to journal on the themes of the 3rd house, such as your relationship with speaking or hearing about challenging topics and how you process information, can help empower you to live a more connected and impactful life in your community.

◆ Understanding the house placement of your 3rd house ruler provides a deeper insight into how you prioritize your community and communication.

◆ Saying or writing "I know" affirmation statements daily will help bring you back to your intellect.

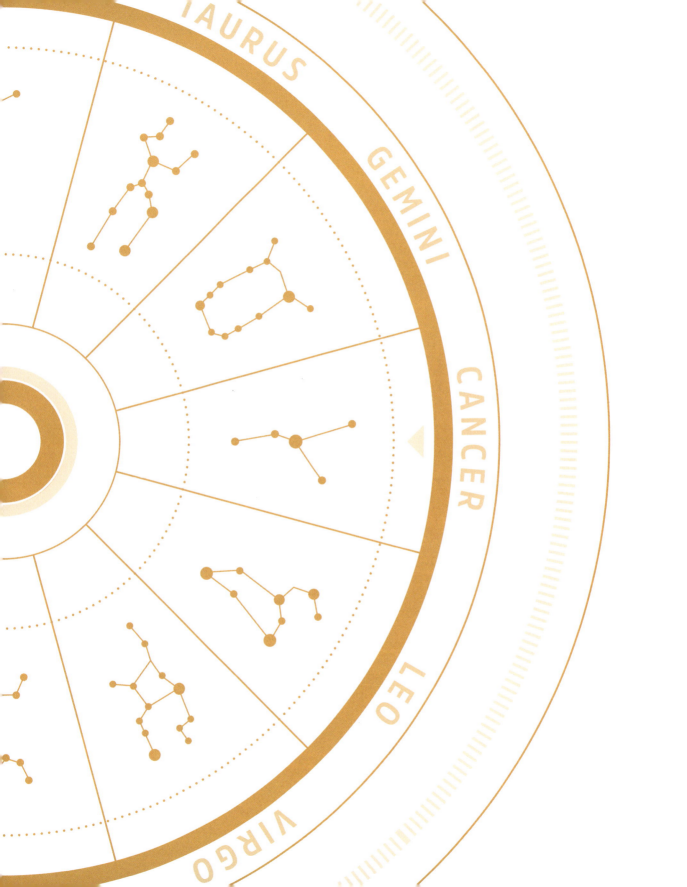

CHAPTER 7

THE 4TH HOUSE OF ASTROLOGY

THE HOUSE OF HOME

In order to understand your psychological foundations, it is important to start by unpacking your relationship to your upbringing, home, and family, which can be found in the 4th house. This is also crucial in understanding the rest of your chart, as it is the key to learning how you process and express your emotions, which are integrally related to every part of your life.

In this chapter, you will learn about the Cancer-ruled 4th house and how it governs your roots, sense of home, and ancestry. Using your birth chart, you will then move through five workbook exercises designed to help you navigate interpreting your chart through the 4th astrological house.

While you can study the general themes of the 4th house and have a good understanding of its meaning, because houses ground your lived experiences, only you can know exactly how this particular area of life shows up for you. The workbook exercises help focus you on the themes of home, safety, security, and nurturing so that you can have a more precise understanding of how you currently experience your 4th house and also where you may still be evolving emotionally.

THE INFLUENCE OF THE 4TH HOUSE

The 4th house is ruled by Cancer and represents your sense of home and ancestry, how you need to be nurtured, and how you nurture others. This is the bottom of your chart, known as the nadir or IC (page 31). It indicates your early childhood and foundations. Much of what is found in the 4th house is in your subconscious and takes emotional maturity and security to fully process and integrate.

There is a focus in this house on your psychological blueprint through your family, especially maternal figures. If you have planets in the 4th house, you may feel either very connected to your family and ancestral lineage or have some wounding in this area of life. As you age, this will result in you being driven to nurture others because you've had to learn how to be a caregiver yourself.

Since the 4th house is associated with ancestry, this is also our connection to history and memories. Our memories store the emotion associated with a time period more than anything else. This part of the chart indicates your emotional core, which developed at a young age. It may be challenging to let go of what has been imprinted here because there is such a deep psychological connection to your associations here, conscious or not.

Learning about your 4th house can help you better understand your psychological foundations and what you need to feel emotionally safe and secure. This requires an ability to be vulnerable and safe within yourself, which can take a lot of work.

YOUR BIRTH CHART

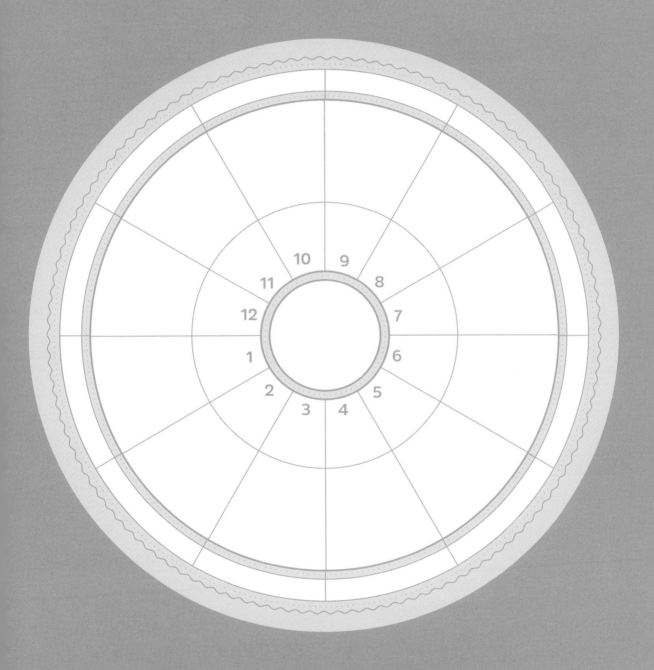

◯ EXERCISE 1

Although the 4th house is naturally ruled by Cancer, your personal birth chart will have a unique zodiac sign flavoring the energy of your 4th house. There may be one or more signs that take up space in your 4th house. The sign that is considered the ruler of your 4th house will be at the beginning of the house, closest to the 3rd house and farthest from the 5th.

Fill in the four blanks at the end of this exercise by following these steps:

1.   Review your birth chart to see what sign rules your 4th house. This is the sign that starts the house.

2.   Use the table on page 42 to see what planet rules that particular sign. This is your 4th house ruling planet. Find that planet in your chart to see in which house it is located.

3.   Use the table to determine the meaning of the house that holds your 4th house ruling planet.

The 4th house in my birth chart is ruled by _____ (sign). The sign that rules my 4th house is ruled by _____ (planet). The planet that rules my personal 4th house is located in the _____ (house) in my birth chart. This house represents _____ (house meaning). My relationship with my parents also shows up in this area of life. Since how I was parented is in this area of life, I also have the greatest potential in this house for unpacking vulnerable parts of my past.

72   The Step-by-Step Astrology Workbook

☾ EXERCISE 2

This exercise will help you understand how your 4th house is influenced by your birth chart placements. In the first column of the following table, circle your 4th house planets. Then read the correlating descriptions in the second column to see how you experience each planet.

4TH HOUSE PLANETS	4TH HOUSE EXPERIENCES
No planets in the 4th house	Review exercise 1 to learn which planet rules your 4th house. Find that planet in your birth chart. The sign that holds this planet will help you understand your 4th house.
Sun	Your identity is intertwined with your childhood experience.
Moon	You have an emotional need to belong. You have strong attachments to your past or ancestors and crave a feeling of home.
Mercury	You have a great memory and are receptive to others' thoughts.
Venus	You need security and comfort and value a feeling of home.
Mars	You release energy through caring for others, especially family.
Jupiter	You may desire a big home, many children, or even a nomadic lifestyle.
Saturn	You likely matured at a young age and may have had a restrictive homelife.
Uranus	You may have grown up in a nontraditional family or be creating one for yourself now.
Neptune	You need to feel connected to your family, but your relationship with them may be quite dynamic and confusing.
Pluto	There may have been power struggles in your family. Your family life is where you have opportunity for transformation.

The 4th House of Astrology   **73**

EXERCISE 3

The Cancer-ruled 4th house represents your subconscious, your family, and what it means to feel at home and nurtured. Use the journal prompts that follow to reflect on the themes of the 4th house.

1. Think about a time when you felt unsafe. What were you able to do that eventually made you feel grounded or secure again? How can you tap into your inner safety daily?

2. What makes you feel nostalgic? Do you feel like you are hanging on to these memories from the past, or are you able to be present with your life today?

3. What makes you feel safe and comfortable? Is it a place, a smell, a feeling? Describe it in detail.

4. Do you have a support system? What makes you feel supported by them? If you don't have one, can you cultivate this feeling for yourself?

5. What makes you feel at home? Describe it in detail.

6. How do you recharge? Do you take enough time daily or weekly to practice what makes you feel rejuvenated?

7. What is the first memory you had as a child? Did you feel hurt by something? Is it a happy memory? Describe it in detail.

8. What does family mean to you?

9. Do you feel in touch with your feelings? Do you have a space where you feel free to express your feelings? What would make you feel safe to express your feelings?

10. What "I feel" statements can you affirm to yourself daily to bring yourself back to feeling emotionally safe and secure? (Examples: *I feel powerful. I feel loved. I feel safe.*)

74   The Step-by-Step Astrology Workbook

EXERCISE 4

In this exercise, you will learn the meaning of the placement of your 4th house ruler. In the following chart, identify your 4th house ruler and read the interpretation. For example, if your 4th house is ruled by Aries, then your 1st house ruler is Mars, so look to see where Mars is in your chart. If you see Mars is in your 4th house, read the 4th house interpretation. Fill in the blanks:

My 4th house ruler is in the _____ (house). This means that my relationship to my home, parents, and ancestry _____ _____.

RULER OF THE 4TH HOUSE IS IN YOUR . . .	MY RELATIONSHIP TO MY HOME, PARENTS, AND ANCESTRY . . .
1st house	influences my identity.
2nd house	is a big component of how I have established my values.
3rd house	is local. I may live near where I grew up or have created something similar.
4th house	is deeply rooted in my subconscious.
5th house	drives my creativity and self-expression.
6th house	makes me feel like I had to grow up fast or take on responsibilities.
7th house	will evolve through my partnerships.
8th house	is related to inheritances or loss.
9th house	is expansive, in that I am always searching for the meaning of home.
10th house	impacts my career and public image.
11th house	may not be the typical definition of family.
12th house	is spiritual and requires me to spend time alone.

The 4th House of Astrology

EXERCISE 5

Respond to the statements in the following self-care checklist to discover whether you are in touch with the themes of the 4th house. If you answer mostly true, you likely already feel empowered in this area of your life. If you answer mostly false, it is nothing to stress about. It simply means you need to focus on this area of life more. It would also be helpful to lean into the qualities of the zodiac sign that is in this area of your chart. The journal prompts in exercise 3 on page 74 and this self-care checklist can support you in your journey of unpacking the themes of this house.

I know what home means to me, and I cultivate that for myself daily.	True	Sometimes True	Sometimes False	False
I have learned my lessons from the past and don't hold on to them.	True	Sometimes True	Sometimes False	False
I know how to identify my feelings and then feel them.	True	Sometimes True	Sometimes False	False
I take time to recharge myself and practice self-care every day.	True	Sometimes True	Sometimes False	False
I have cultivated a support system that makes me feel safe and secure.	True	Sometimes True	Sometimes False	False
Even if I have others to support me, I know how to nurture myself.	True	Sometimes True	Sometimes False	False
Cleaning or reorganizing my physical space helps give me space to process emotions.	True	Sometimes True	Sometimes False	False
I let myself cry.	True	Sometimes True	Sometimes False	False

The Step-by-Step Astrology Workbook

KEY TAKEAWAYS

Understanding and unpacking how you experience the 4th house of home and ancestry gives insight into your subconscious programming, early childhood, and deeply rooted foundations.

- ◆ The 4th house represents the psychological blueprint established through your early childhood education experiences, family, and ancestral lineage. Healing this part of your subconscious requires practice being vulnerable, nurturing, and taking care of yourself.

- ◆ The planets represent an aspect of your personality. Any planets located in the 4th house influence your subconscious and provide an additional layer of how you process emotions, your relationship with your parents, and your feelings around home.

- ◆ An individual's relationship with their upbringing is complex and unique to them. Taking time to journal on the themes of the 4th house, such as safety, childhood memories, and how you have or haven't been allowed to process your feelings, can help empower you to safely express your deepest emotions.

- ◆ Understanding the house placement of your 4th house ruler provides a deeper insight into your relationships to your home, parents, and ancestry.

- ◆ Saying or writing "I feel" affirmation statements daily will help bring you back to feeling emotionally safe and secure.

The 4th House of Astrology   77

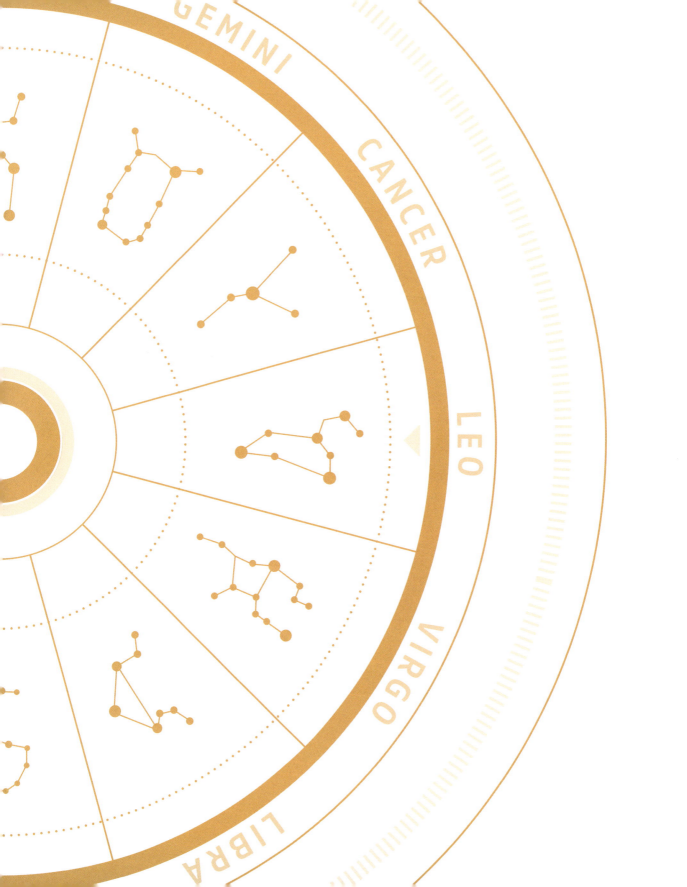

CHAPTER 8

THE 5TH HOUSE OF ASTROLOGY

THE HOUSE OF PLEASURE

In order to understand how you can best express yourself authentically, it is important to start by learning about where you find pleasure most easily, which can be located in the 5th house. This also supports you in understanding other areas of your chart, as it represents your creativity and passion, which are necessary components of many human experiences.

In this chapter, you will learn about the Leo-ruled 5th house and how it governs the inner child, creativity, and passion. Using your birth chart, you will then move through five workbook exercises designed to help you navigate interpreting your chart through the 5th astrological house.

While you can study the general themes of the 5th house and have a good understanding of its meaning, because houses ground your lived experiences, only you can know exactly how this particular area of life shows up for you. The workbook exercises help focus you on the themes of self-expression, inner confidence, and what you do for fun, so that you can have a more precise understanding of how you currently experience your 5th house and also where you may need to bring a little more pleasure into your life.

THE INFLUENCE OF THE 5TH HOUSE

The 5th house is ruled by Leo and represents creativity, children, hobbies, entertainment, and anything you do for fun. This is the area of your life where you take risks and put yourself out there. You may have a childlike wonder here, more passion, more drama, and certainly a bigger heart.

If you have planets in the 5th house, this indicates there is a focus on creativity and taking risks. If you think about a child, they are typically expressive and unashamed, regardless of how loud, silly, or passionate they are. A strong 5th house may indicate that you put yourself out there, perhaps onstage or in the way you dress. Many actors have strong 5th house placements.

Everyone is creative, just in their own way. The 5th house is where you can harness your unique creativity and create simply for pleasure rather than for an intended outcome. This is where you may feel more passionate or seek pleasure and joy. You get to express yourself fully here and be unashamed, although depending on placements in your 5th house, you may feel self-conscious in the process.

The 5th house is where you have the opportunity to do inner-child work. Does your inner child still express itself fully now that you've been influenced by society, or do you need to nurture your inner joy and passion for life? This area of the chart is heart-led and does not want you to compromise living your fullest expression of self.

YOUR BIRTH CHART

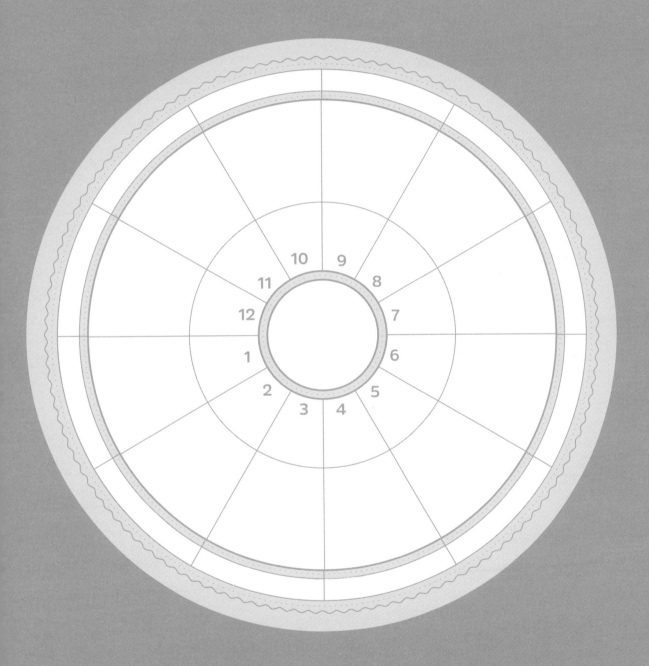

◯ EXERCISE 1

Although the 5th house is naturally ruled by Taurus, your personal birth chart will have a unique zodiac sign flavoring the energy of your 5th house. There may be one or more signs that take up space in your 5th house. The sign that is considered the ruler of your 5th house will be at the beginning of the house, closest to the 4th house and farthest from the 6th.

Fill in the four blanks at the end of this exercise by following these steps:

1. Review your birth chart to see what sign rules your 5th house. This is the sign that starts the house.

2. Use the table on page 42 to see what planet rules that particular sign. This is your 5th house ruling planet. Find that planet in your chart to see in which house it is located.

3. Use the table to determine the meaning of the house that holds your 5th house ruling planet.

The 5th house in my birth chart is ruled by _____ (sign). The sign that rules my 5th house is ruled by _____ (planet). The planet that rules my personal 5th house is located in the _____ (house) in my birth chart. This house represents _____ (house meaning). My inner child also shows up in this area of life. Since my inner child shows up in this area of life, I also have the greatest potential for learning how to let go and have fun.

☾ EXERCISE 2

This exercise will help you understand how your 5th house is influenced by your birth chart placements. In the first column of the following table, circle your 5th house planets. Then read the correlating descriptions in the second column to see how you experience each planet.

5TH HOUSE PLANETS	5TH HOUSE EXPERIENCES
No planets in the 5th house	Review exercise 1 to learn which planet rules your 5th house. Find that planet in your birth chart. The sign that holds this planet will help you understand your 5th house.
Sun	You have a playful heart and are meant to express yourself, no matter how dramatic it may seem.
Moon	You have an emotional need to truly feel seen. You are expressive and playful with your feelings and sometimes need to take them seriously.
Mercury	You like to use your words to express yourself creatively.
Venus	You need to feel playful and creative, and you value self-expression.
Mars	You release energy through creativity and play.
Jupiter	You are passionate about travel and new experiences.
Saturn	You may have had to grow up quickly, without being able to enjoy being a child. You likely take relationships or parenthood seriously.
Uranus	You need to feel that you can express your uniqueness and have a need for freedom in relationships.
Neptune	You are a romantic and have a dreamy vision for your family life.
Pluto	You are passionate in relationships and need to be aware of potential control issues.

The 5th House of Astrology   **83**

EXERCISE 3

The Leo-ruled 5th house represents your creativity, your passion and romance, and your inner child. Use the journal prompts that follow to reflect on the themes of the 5th house.

1. Think about a time when you felt free to express yourself. How did it feel? Do you always feel this way?

2. What do you love to create? You don't have to be artistic. You are a creator of something. How can you lean into this more?

3. What part of your life do you put on a pedestal? Does it deserve to be there? What else needs to get more attention or praise in your life?

4. How can you feel proud of yourself even if you don't feel like everything is going right?

5. Find an old photo of yourself from childhood. What do you remember about this time in your life? Is there any hurt?

6. How would you talk to yourself if you were able to speak to yourself as a child? What would you tell yourself?

7. What did you need as a child that you didn't get (for example, resources or love)? How can you give that to yourself today?

8. What did you do for fun as a child? Can you do that today? What else can you do simply for pleasure?

9. What is something that gives you pure pleasure in life? Are you doing enough of it? How can you make time for feeling good?

10. Write a list of 100 things you like about yourself. Put it in a place you see regularly.

EXERCISE 4

In this exercise, you will learn the meaning of the placement of your 5th house ruler. In the following chart, identify your 5th house ruler and read the interpretation. For example, if your 5th house is ruled by Taurus, then your 5th house ruler is Venus. Then, look to see where Venus is in your chart. If you see Venus is in your 4th house, read the 4th house interpretation. Fill in the blanks:

My 5th house ruler is in the _____ (house). This means that my relationship to pleasure, fun, and creativity _____
_____.

RULER OF THE 5TH HOUSE IS IN YOUR...	MY RELATIONSHIP TO PLEASURE, FUN, AND CREATIVITY...
1st house	is all about being true to myself.
2nd house	is related to my sense of worth and financial security.
3rd house	is found in my local community and through my words.
4th house	may be aligned with my family or be best expressed at home.
5th house	is a key component of my life and comes easily to me.
6th house	requires intention, organization, and structure.
7th house	is best expressed through my relationship with others.
8th house	allows me to tap into my subconscious.
9th house	allows me to feel free.
10th house	is part of my career and public image.
11th house	is best expressed through my community.
12th house	is something I like to do in isolation, to go inward.

The 5th House of Astrology

EXERCISE 5

Respond to the statements in the following self-care checklist to discover whether you are in touch with the themes of the 5th house. If you answer mostly true, you likely already feel empowered in this area of your life. If you answer mostly false, it is nothing to stress about. It simply means you need to focus on this area of life more. It would also be helpful to lean into the qualities of the zodiac sign that is in this area of your chart. The journal prompts in exercise 3 on page 84 and this self-care checklist can support you in your journey of unpacking the themes of this house.

I take time daily or weekly to do something just for pleasure.	True	Sometimes True	Sometimes False	False
I incorporate something fun into every day.	True	Sometimes True	Sometimes False	False
I know how to express my creativity.	True	Sometimes True	Sometimes False	False
I am not afraid to express myself, and I do so confidently.	True	Sometimes True	Sometimes False	False
I know what I did not get as a child and provide that to myself now.	True	Sometimes True	Sometimes False	False
I feel proud to be exactly who I am, regardless of what anyone else thinks or says.	True	Sometimes True	Sometimes False	False
I know what my heart wants, and I follow it.	True	Sometimes True	Sometimes False	False
I am actively working to feel worthy in the parts of my personality that I am self-conscious about. I am worthy.	True	Sometimes True	Sometimes False	False

The Step-by-Step Astrology Workbook

KEY TAKEAWAYS

Understanding and unpacking how you experience the 5th house of creativity and children can help you find your inner joy and passion in life.

◆ The 5th house represents your ability to lead from your heart, regardless of what others think. It is where you can understand true pleasure through passion, rather than acting with an intended outcome.

◆ The planets represent an aspect of your personality. Any planets located in the 5th house influence your joy, passion, and pleasure and provide an additional layer of how you can lead from your heart and not compromise on living your fullest expression of self.

◆ An individual's relationship with their inner child is complex and unique to them. Taking time to journal on the themes of the 5th house, such as self-expression, creativity, and what you can do for fun, can help empower you to live from a place of pure joy and passion.

◆ Understanding the house placement of your 5th house ruler provides a deeper insight into your relationship to pleasure, fun, and creativity.

◆ Writing a list of 100 things you like about yourself and posting it in a place where you will see it daily will help you love yourself for who you are at your core.

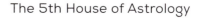

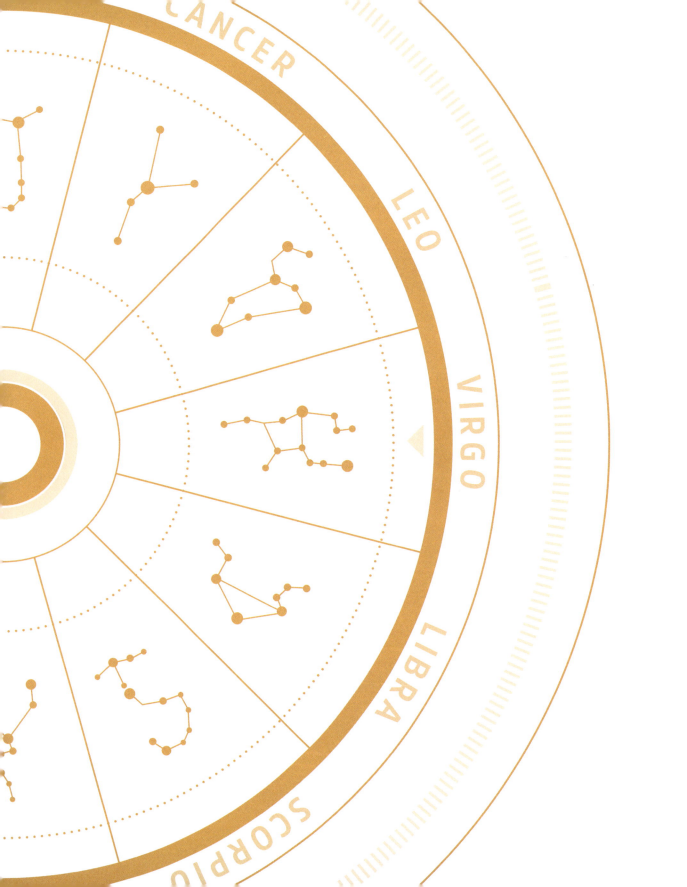

CHAPTER 9

THE 6TH HOUSE OF ASTROLOGY

THE HOUSE OF HEALTH

To dive deep into understanding your best way to live a healthy lifestyle, it is important to start by unpacking your daily routines and unique vitality, which can be found in the 6th house. Your daily routines, including daily habits, hobbies, and maintaining schedules, are key to understanding your chart as a whole, as where you spend your time minute to minute impacts your entire well-being.

In this chapter, you will learn about the Virgo-ruled 6th house and how it governs vitality, well-being, and daily routines. Using your birth chart, you will then move through five workbook exercises designed to help you navigate interpreting your chart through the 6th astrological house.

While you can study the general themes of the 6th house and have a good understanding of its meaning, because houses ground your lived experiences, only you can know exactly how this particular area of life shows up for you. The workbook exercises help focus you on the themes of healthy habits and routines, as well as your relationship with time and resources. Moving through these exercises will support you in having a more precise understanding of how you currently experience your 6th house and also where you have room to add or remove particular daily habits.

THE INFLUENCE OF THE 6TH HOUSE

The 6th house is ruled by Virgo and represents your general health, pets, and the work that you complete out of necessity. It also rules natural health strategies and preventative remedies such as herbs, yoga, and updates to your daily routines. Understanding the 6th house of health is crucial to supporting the rest of your chart, as it can empower you to listen to your own unique rhythms.

If you have planets in the 6th house, it is likely that your personal health and supporting others on their health journey is a big theme in your life. It is not uncommon for charts with strong 6th house placements to undergo their own health challenges as a means to learn to heal themselves. Part of their purpose is to then support others through their own healing processes. Often, it becomes the employment through which they receive income.

Since the 6th house is associated with day-to-day life, it is where we can find our relationship with the more mundane aspects of life. This includes daily tasks and decisions at work and in the home, such as what to wear each day, when to feed the dog, taking out the trash, and exercising.

Ultimately, the placements of your 6th house indicate your rhythm of daily doings, your relationship with time and resources, and how well you are taking care of yourself. Learning about your 6th house can help you better understand where you may need to spend more or less time and energy.

YOUR BIRTH CHART

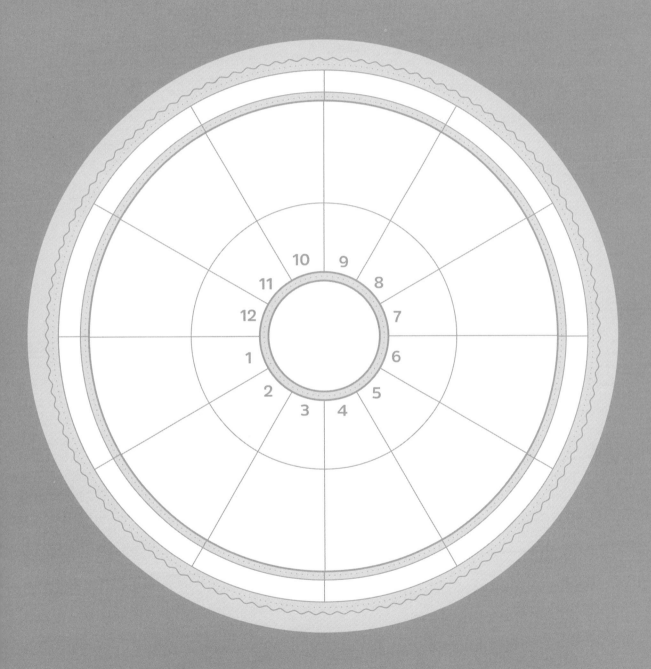

◯ EXERCISE 1

Although the 6th house is naturally ruled by Virgo, your personal birth chart will have a unique zodiac sign flavoring the energy of your 6th house. There may be one or more signs that take up space in your 6th house. The sign that is considered the ruler of your 6th house will be at the beginning of the house, closest to the 5th house and farthest from the 7th.

Fill in the four blanks at the end of this exercise following these steps:

1. Review your birth chart to see what sign rules your 6th house. This is the sign that starts the house.

2. Use the table on page 42 to see what planet rules that particular sign. This is your 6th house ruling planet. Find that planet in your chart to see in which house it is located.

3. Use the table to determine the meaning of the house that holds your 6th house ruling planet.

The 6th house in my birth chart is ruled by _____ (sign). The sign that rules my 6th house is ruled by _____ (planet). The planet that rules my personal 6th house is located in the _____ (house) in my birth chart. This house represents _____ (house meaning). My relationship with time and resources also shows up in this area of life. I have great potential for learning how to spend my time and energy in ways that best support my overall health.

92   *The Step-by-Step Astrology Workbook*

(EXERCISE 2

This exercise will help you understand how your 6th house is influenced by your birth chart placements. In the first column of the following table, circle your 6th house planets. Then read the correlating descriptions in the second column to see how you experience each planet.

6TH HOUSE PLANETS	6TH HOUSE EXPERIENCES
No planets in the 6th house	Review exercise 1 to learn which planet rules your 6th house. Find that planet in your birth chart. The sign that holds this planet will help you understand your 6th house.
Sun	Your identity and self-expression are caught up in day-to-day doings. You are attracted to healing yourself and others.
Moon	You have an emotional need to be productive. If you do not attend to your emotional body, you may experience health issues.
Mercury	You are great with details and facts. You can compartmentalize.
Venus	You value self-improvement and acts of service.
Mars	You put energy into getting things done and can achieve a lot.
Jupiter	You can conquer any task, even big jobs. You take your health to extremes.
Saturn	You are serious about doing things well. You may tend to enforce restrictions around your diet or exercise.
Uranus	You have an unusual daily routine and don't like being told what to do.
Neptune	You feel physical health on an unconscious level.
Pluto	You may have a power struggle with health or work.

The 6th House of Astrology   **93**

☽ EXERCISE 3

The Virgo-ruled 6th house represents your daily routines, tasks, and general health. The goal is to incorporate daily routines that support your overall well-being and that ultimately allow you to be of service to others. Though the 6th house can feel mundane, it is crucial to your healing process. Use the journal prompts that follow to reflect on the themes of the 6th house.

1. What is work-life balance? ("Work" can be a career or any daily tasks that constitute work.) What does it mean to you? Do you feel that you have work-life balance?

2. Where are you critical of yourself? How can you be kinder to yourself?

3. When do you tend to be critical of others? Is this coming from your own way of doing things or your own version of what is "perfect"?

4. What is something you love about your daily routine? Do you actually make sure you do it every day?

5. What is something you dislike about your daily routine? Can you make it more enjoyable or remove it altogether?

6. What do you enjoy helping people with—in other words, how do you serve others? In what ways can you serve others more?

7. How do you react when someone offers to help you? Are you able to receive help?

8. What does relaxing look like to you? How can you incorporate more of this into your daily routine?

9. What do you do that prioritizes your health? What else would make you feel good?

10. Write a to-do list. What can you cross off immediately? Where can you ask for help?

EXERCISE 4

In this exercise, you will learn the meaning of the placement of your 6th house ruler. In the following chart, identify your 6th house ruler and read the interpretation. For example, if your 6th house is ruled by Leo, then your 6th house ruler is the Sun, so look to see where the Sun is in your chart. If you see the Sun is in your 6th house, read the 6th house interpretation. Fill in the blanks:

My 6th house ruler is in the _____ (house). This means that when I am disciplined and focused on _____ _____ I feel more effective and healthier.

RULER OF THE 6TH HOUSE IS IN YOUR...	I FEEL MORE EFFECTIVE AND HEALTHY WHEN I AM DISCIPLINED AND FOCUSED ON...
1st house	my physical body and vitality.
2nd house	keeping a budget and generating income and resources.
3rd house	keeping my word and focusing on my community.
4th house	maintaining a stable and secure home and family life.
5th house	expressing my creativity and being playful.
6th house	keeping my life, and likely others' lives, organized.
7th house	balance in relationships.
8th house	taking care of my inner wounds and emotional body.
9th house	expanding my mind through travel or spirituality.
10th house	my professional or public life.
11th house	my connection to friends.
12th house	my unconscious.

The 6th House of Astrology

EXERCISE 5

Respond to the statements in the following self-care checklist to discover whether you are in touch with the themes of the 6th house. If you answer mostly true, you likely already feel empowered in this area of your life. If you answer mostly false, it is nothing to stress about. It simply means you need to focus on this area of life more. It would also be helpful to lean into the qualities of the zodiac sign that is in this area of your chart. The journal prompts in exercise 3 on page 94 and this self-care checklist can support you in your journey of unpacking the themes of this house.

I have a daily routine that supports my mental, physical, and spiritual health.	True	Sometimes True	Sometimes False	False
I create space for flexibility in my daily routine.	True	Sometimes True	Sometimes False	False
I take care of my body by moving it in a way that feels good and supporting it with nourishing food.	True	Sometimes True	Sometimes False	False
I am not overly critical of myself, and I speak kindly to myself.	True	Sometimes True	Sometimes False	False
I am not overly critical or judgmental of others.	True	Sometimes True	Sometimes False	False
I am able to ask for and accept help when needed.	True	Sometimes True	Sometimes False	False
I am easily able to prioritize what is most important in the moment.	True	Sometimes True	Sometimes False	False
I have a good work-life balance and feel fulfilled in both aspects.	True	Sometimes True	Sometimes False	False

KEY TAKEAWAYS

Understanding and unpacking how you experience the 6th house of health can help you have a deeper sense of how you can best support your vitality through your daily routines and work ethic.

◆ The 6th house represents your general health, work, and routines. Understanding this part of your chart can give you insight into where you may need to spend more or less time and energy to feel healthy and productive.

◆ The planets represent an aspect of your personality. Any planets located in the 6th house influence your vitality and provide an additional layer of how you can best support your health.

◆ An individual's general well-being and vitality are complex and unique to them. Taking time to journal on the themes of the 6th house, such as work-life balance and what you do and don't love about your daily routine, can help empower you to live a life aligned with what makes you feel good.

◆ Understanding the house placement of your 6th house ruler provides a deeper insight into what you need to be focused on in order to feel more effective and healthy.

◆ Practicing writing a to-do list and determining both what you can do and what you can ask for assistance with can help you feel more energized by your daily tasks.

The 6th House of Astrology

CHAPTER 10

THE 7TH HOUSE OF ASTROLOGY

THE HOUSE OF RELATIONSHIPS

The 7th house is the first house that shifts into relating to others, and it is foundational in understanding all forms of one-on-one relationships. The 7th house helps you understand how you can seek balance in relating to others and is crucial to understanding how your identity shifts while collaborating with someone who thinks and feels differently from you.

In this chapter, you will learn about the Libra-ruled 7th house and how it governs marriage, romantic partnerships, and business partnerships—and also enemies. Using your birth chart, you will then move through five workbook exercises designed to help you navigate interpreting your chart through the 7th astrological house.

While you can study the general themes of the 7th house and have a good understanding of its meaning, because houses ground your lived experiences, only you can know exactly how this particular area of life shows up for you. The workbook exercises help focus you on what informs your relationships, how you show up in relationships, and what your needs are in a relationship, so that you can have a more precise understanding of how you currently experience your 7th house and also where you have room to grow.

THE INFLUENCE OF THE 7TH HOUSE

The 7th house is ruled by Libra and represents one-on-one relationships, including marriage, romantic partnerships, business partnerships, and enemies. It is where you can find out how you relate to others, including how you balance each relationship with your own inner balance. The 7th house also represents your aesthetic taste, potential artistic abilities, contracts, legalities, and your negotiation tactics.

As the first house in the second half of the wheel, the 7th house is where we shift from self toward the other. In this case, "the other" is a partner, but you'll notice all of the houses moving forward are shifted toward different versions of the other. Through partnership, we understand ourselves in a new way. In the 7th house, you can discover why you seek, or don't seek, partnership; how you find fulfillment through partnership; what lessons you are meant to learn through partnership; and where you are more likely to create enemies instead.

Since the 7th house is directly opposite your 1st house, the sign that rules the 7th house in your natal chart will always be in polarity with your rising sign. In other words, qualities associated with the sign opposite your rising are what you may find you are in fact attracted to and fill a need in your life. This is why you may find that opposites attract romantically or in business partnership.

Though the 7th house is about the other, in actuality it wants you to find inner balance first. This is the key to a successful romantic or business relationship.

YOUR BIRTH CHART

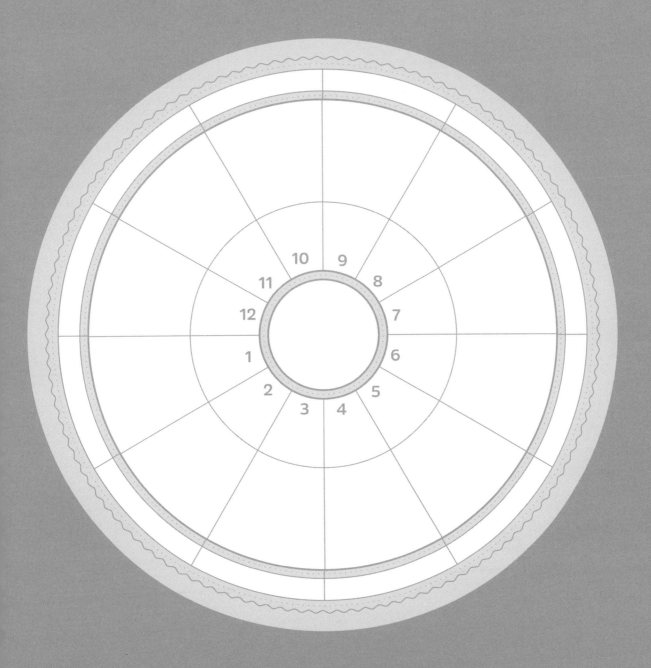

◯ EXERCISE 1

Although the 7th house is naturally ruled by Libra, your personal birth chart will have a unique zodiac sign flavoring the energy of your 7th house. There may be one or more signs that take up space in your 7th house. The sign that is considered the ruler of your 7th house will be at the beginning of the house, closest to the 6th house and farthest from the 8th.

Fill in the four blanks at the end of this exercise by following these steps:

1. Review your birth chart to see what sign rules your 7th house. This is the sign that starts the house.

2. Use the table on page 42 to see what planet rules that particular sign. This is your 7th house ruling planet. Find that planet in your chart to see in which house it is located.

3. Use the table to determine the meaning of the house that holds your 7th house ruling planet.

The 7th house in my birth chart is ruled by _____ (sign). The sign that rules my 7th house is ruled by _____ (planet). The planet that rules my personal 7th house is located in the _____ (house) in my birth chart. This house represents _____ (house meaning). My inner balance also shows up in this area of life. Since my inner balance shows up in this area of life, I also have the opportunity to find inner peace here, ultimately supporting my relationships with others.

102   The Step-by-Step Astrology Workbook

(EXERCISE 2

This exercise will help you understand how your 7th house is influenced by your birth chart placements. In the first column of the following table, circle your 7th house planets. Then read the correlating descriptions in the second column to see how you experience each planet.

7TH HOUSE PLANETS	7TH HOUSE EXPERIENCES
No planets in the 7th house	Review exercise 1 to learn which planet rules your 7th house. Find that planet in your birth chart. The sign that holds this planet will help you understand your 7th house.
Sun	Your identity and self-expression shine through in partnership. You care about balance, which also means you put your own needs last.
Moon	You are drawn to living life in partnership, and you seek balance emotionally.
Mercury	You are a natural mediator and connector.
Venus	You look for the best in people and are a natural negotiator.
Mars	You pour energy into partnerships but may come off as aggressive.
Jupiter	You seek freedom and fun in relationships.
Saturn	You take relationships seriously and seek maturity.
Uranus	You may have an unconventional relationship and need independence.
Neptune	You may be a hopeless romantic and are learning boundaries in relationships.
Pluto	You seek transformation through relationships and come across power struggles.

The 7th House of Astrology   103

☽ EXERCISE 3

The Libra-ruled 7th house represents how you relate to others, especially romantically and in business partnerships. The goal is for you to find inner balance within yourself first, and then find harmony in partnership. It is important not to give more than you receive—or vice versa. Since it is the 7th house, it also represents all things beautiful and aesthetically pleasing. Use the journal prompts that follow to reflect on the themes of the 7th house.

1. Do you give your energy away to others? How often? Does this make you feel good or drained?

2. How do you find inner balance? Do you practice coming into balance every day?

3. What do you seek in partnership that you don't see in yourself?

4. Where do you use partnership as a crutch? How can you cultivate this energy for yourself?

5. What does beauty mean to you? What about inner beauty? How can you create more beauty around you every day?

6. Where are you indecisive? What would help you make decisions in this area of life?

7. When it comes to conflict, how do you typically engage? Does this work for you, or is there room for improvement?

8. What does being social mean to you? Do you have enough time in your day or week to incorporate social activities that you enjoy?

9. How can you deepen your relationships with others in your life?

10. What is your love language? How can you show this type of love to yourself?

104   *The Step-by-Step Astrology Workbook*

EXERCISE 4

In this exercise, you will learn the meaning of the placement of your 7th house ruler. In the following chart, identify your 7th house ruler and read the interpretation. For example, if your 7th house is ruled by Aries, then your 7th house ruler is Mars, so look to see where Mars is in your chart. If you see Mars is in your 8th house, read the 8th house interpretation. Fill in the blanks:

My 7th house ruler is in the _____ (house). This means that in one-on-one partnerships, I _____
_____.

RULER OF THE 7TH HOUSE IS IN YOUR...	IN ONE-ON-ONE PARTNERSHIPS, I...
1st house	am exploring my identity.
2nd house	need security and stability, especially financially.
3rd house	am inclined to partner with someone I grew up with.
4th house	need to feel like I'm at home or re-create my own version of home.
5th house	am playful and need to feel free to express myself.
6th house	am practical and disciplined.
7th house	need balance and harmony.
8th house	crave depth and intimacy.
9th house	need freedom and the ability to continue learning.
10th house	desire to be a power couple.
11th house	want to date or marry my best friend.
12th house	need alone time and to be connected spiritually.

The 7th House of Astrology

EXERCISE 5

Respond to the statements in the following self-care checklist to discover whether you are in touch with the themes of the 7th house. If you answer mostly true, you likely already feel empowered in this area of your life. If you answer mostly false, it is nothing to stress about. It simply means you need to focus on this area of life more. It would also be helpful to lean into the qualities of the zodiac sign that is in this area of your chart. The journal prompts in exercise 3 on page 104 and this self-care checklist can support you in your journey of unpacking the themes of this house.

I have consistent access to inner balance.	True	Sometimes True	Sometimes False	False
Though I may value partnership, I know I am worthy without a partner.	True	Sometimes True	Sometimes False	False
I can make authentic decisions for myself and do not make them based off how someone else may feel.	True	Sometimes True	Sometimes False	False
I support myself as much as I support others. I am neither selfish nor selfless.	True	Sometimes True	Sometimes False	False
I approach conflict by seeking a result that does not compromise either party.	True	Sometimes True	Sometimes False	False
I have a balanced social life and also take time to rest.	True	Sometimes True	Sometimes False	False
I can find beauty in all areas of life.	True	Sometimes True	Sometimes False	False
I do not give my power away in relationships; I am empowered with or without a partner.	True	Sometimes True	Sometimes False	False

106   The Step-by-Step Astrology Workbook

KEY TAKEAWAYS

Understanding and unpacking how you experience the 7th house of relationships can help you have a deeper sense of your romantic and business partnerships.

- ◆ The 7th house represents your one-on-one relationships, including marriage, business partners, and enemies. Understanding this part of your chart can give you insight into how you relate to others.

- ◆ The planets represent an aspect of your personality. Any planets located in the 7th house influence your approach to relationships and how you may find balance within partnership.

- ◆ An individual's approach to and experience within a relationship is complex and unique to them. Taking time to journal on the themes of the 7th house, such as how you engage with conflict and how you can cultivate inner balance, can help empower you to show up authentically in a relationship.

- ◆ Understanding the house placement of your 7th house ruler provides a deeper insight into what you need to be focused on in order to feel fulfilled in a relationship.

- ◆ Understanding your love language and determining how you can provide this love to yourself can help you meet your own needs and express them effectively in partnerships.

CHAPTER 11

THE 8TH HOUSE OF ASTROLOGY

THE HOUSE OF SEX & DEATH

The 8th house is one of the most easily misunderstood houses, as it unpacks topics that are generally taboo, such as the occult, things hidden, death, loss, taxes, and inheritances. While it may not feel comfortable, it is crucial to unpack your 8th house, as it represents everything you bury deep within your psyche and therefore is underlying how you process every other area of life.

In this chapter, you will learn about the Scorpio-ruled 8th house and how it governs death and rebirth, sexuality, and merging with others. Using your birth chart, you will then move through five workbook exercises designed to help you navigate interpreting your chart through the 8th astrological house.

While you can study the general themes of the 8th house and have a good understanding of its meaning, because houses ground your lived experiences, only you can know exactly how this particular area of life shows up for you. The workbook exercises help focus you on the themes of loss, transformation, and inheritances, so that you can have a more precise understanding of your psychological makeup and where you can move forward in your personal development journey.

THE INFLUENCE OF THE 8TH HOUSE

The 8th house is ruled by Scorpio and represents transformation, crisis, death and rebirth, sexuality, and personal growth. It rules all things that many people are less comfortable talking about publicly and likely keep hidden or are only open about in intimate relationships. The 8th house indicates where we merge; therefore, it also represents other people's money, estates, taxes, and inheritances.

Everything found in the 8th house requires death and rebirth, a complete undoing in order to transform into the highest potential. Since this can feel so monumental and often exhausting, it is common to want to control this part of your life and keep it from constantly going into crisis mode. As a result, you can find your attitude toward change here as well.

This part of the chart is where you keep deep psychological parts of yourself hidden from others, and often even hidden from your conscious self. This is why your 8th house placements and rulership can be a strong indicator of where you may benefit from therapy or other deep healing tools. If you have planets in the 8th house, you may feel like you are constantly healing and transforming, or you may be a therapist or healer yourself.

It is not uncommon to have a sense of fear of the 8th house, mostly because of our attachment to the old and fear of transformative growth. It always requires change, so you must learn to let go of these parts of yourself to truly emerge into your highest potential.

YOUR BIRTH CHART

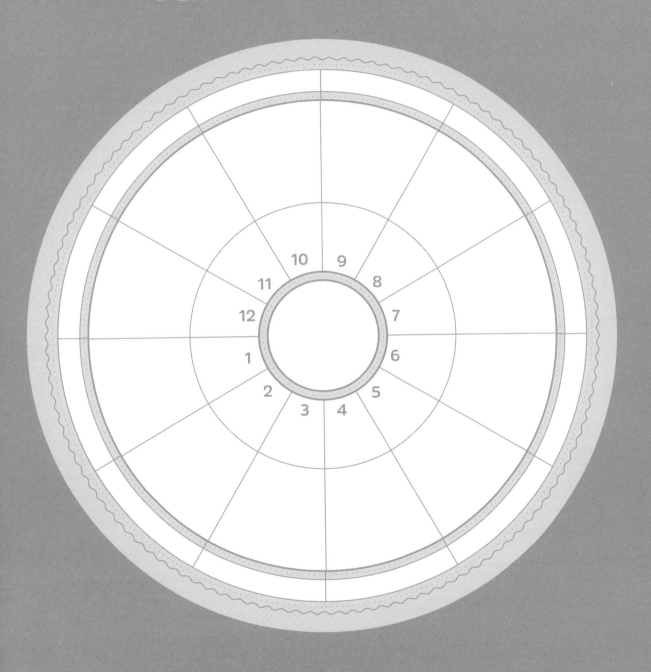

◯ EXERCISE 1

Although the 8th house is naturally ruled by Scorpio, your personal birth chart will have a unique zodiac sign flavoring the energy of your 8th house. There may be one or more signs that take up space in your 8th house. The sign that is considered the ruler of your 8th house will be at the beginning of the house, closest to the 7th house and farthest from the 9th.

Fill in the four blanks at the end of this exercise by following these steps:

1. Review your birth chart to see what sign rules your 8th house. This is the sign that starts the house.

2. Use the table on page 42 to see what planet rules that particular sign. This is your 8th house ruling planet. Find that planet in your chart to see in which house it is located.

3. Use the table to determine the meaning of the house that holds your 8th house ruling planet.

The 8th house in my birth chart is ruled by _____ (sign). The sign that rules my 8th house is ruled by _____ (planet). The planet that rules my personal 8th house is located in the _____ (house) in my birth chart. This house represents _____ (house meaning). The parts of my psyche that I keep hidden even from myself are also found here. Since my subconscious self shows up in this area of life, I also have the greatest potential for letting go and healing.

☾ EXERCISE 2

This exercise will help you understand how your 8th house is influenced by your birth chart placements. In the first column of the following table, circle your 8th house planets. Then read the correlating descriptions in the second column to see how you experience each planet.

8TH HOUSE PLANETS	8TH HOUSE EXPERIENCES
No planets in the 8th house	Review exercise 1 to learn which planet rules your 8th house. Find that planet in your birth chart. The sign that holds this planet will help you understand your 8th house.
Sun	You constantly explore your identity and seek self-transformation and growth.
Moon	You need emotional security but tend to have a hard time letting people in.
Mercury	Your mind is intuitive and you understand the psychology behind someone's motivations.
Venus	You want a deep connection and value vulnerability.
Mars	You are deeply passionate and seek control.
Jupiter	You may have luck with inheritances or money from others. You are optimistic with the dark parts of life.
Saturn	You likely have difficulty letting go of anything. You may have experienced loss at a young age.
Uranus	You may not desire commitment, and you may have ups and downs or have unconventional ways of handling taxes or inheritances.
Neptune	There may be confusion or lack of memory around 8th house themes. Be compassionate with yourself.
Pluto	You have powerful intimate relationships. Pay attention to power struggles and control.

The 8th House of Astrology   113

EXERCISE 3

The Scorpio-ruled 8th house represents death and rebirth; it is pure transformative energy. The goal is to trust yourself enough to go to the deepest and darkest parts of your psyche and transform into your highest potential. Use the journal prompts that follow to reflect on the themes of the 8th house.

1. What is change? How do you feel when something in your life changes?

2. What is control? What do you feel the need to have control over in your life?

3. Where do you need to let go of control? How does letting go of control make you feel?

4. Do you trust yourself? Where are you seeking outside advice? How can you cultivate this support within yourself?

5. What is something challenging that sticks out from your childhood? How is this emotion still present in your life today? How can you transform this into your superpower?

6. Do you easily trust others, or does it take a long time for you to trust? What happens when your trust is broken?

7. Where do you feel like you are constantly in crisis mode? How can you take a step back and let things move forward on their own?

8. What is your relationship with sexual energy? Do you feel free to express yourself sexually? Is there anyone you can trust enough to be fully intimate with?

9. Do you have any inheritances? How do you think having or not having this has impacted your relationship with money?

10. What are your deepest, darkest secrets? Who do you share them with? Are you still healing from them?

114 *The Step-by-Step Astrology Workbook*

EXERCISE 4

In this exercise, you will learn the meaning of the placement of your 8th house ruler. In the following chart, identify your 8th house ruler and read the interpretation. For example, if your 8th house is ruled by Capricorn, then your 8th house ruler is Saturn, so look to see where Saturn is in your chart. If you see Saturn is in your 4th house, read the 4th house interpretation. Fill in the blanks:

My 8th house ruler is in the _____ (house). This means that I can learn more about my relationship with power and transform through _____ _____.

RULER OF THE 8TH HOUSE IS IN YOUR...	I CAN LEARN MORE ABOUT MY RELATIONSHIP WITH POWER AND TRANSFORM THROUGH...
1st house	understanding my identity and claiming my agency.
2nd house	my relationship to money and resources.
3rd house	understanding my role in my community.
4th house	exploring my ancestry and lineage.
5th house	tapping into my creativity and self-expression.
6th house	understanding why I feel responsible for others.
7th house	finding myself in a relationship.
8th house	healthily handling grief.
9th house	seeking my own truth.
10th house	understanding my role in the public eye.
11th house	understanding what impact I can make on humanity.
12th house	feeling comfortable in isolation.

The 8th House of Astrology

EXERCISE 5

Respond to the statements in the following self-care checklist to discover whether you are in touch with the themes of the 8th house. If you answer mostly true, you likely already feel empowered in this area of your life. If you answer mostly false, it is nothing to stress about. It simply means you need to focus on this area of life more. It would also be helpful to lean into the qualities of the zodiac sign that is in this area of your chart. The journal prompts in exercise 3 on page 114 and this self-care checklist can support you in your journey of unpacking the themes of this house.

I do not try to control the people in my life.	True	Sometimes True	Sometimes False	False
I am comfortable letting go of control and trusting that things will all work out.	True	Sometimes True	Sometimes False	False
I trust myself to know what is correct in the moment.	True	Sometimes True	Sometimes False	False
I know that change is inevitable and trust that I will grow from it.	True	Sometimes True	Sometimes False	False
I neither overly trust others nor completely distrust others. I have a healthy amount of trust toward others.	True	Sometimes True	Sometimes False	False
I have a positive relationship with my sexual energy.	True	Sometimes True	Sometimes False	False
Though I may have had challenges in childhood and am still healing, I know how to continue to heal.	True	Sometimes True	Sometimes False	False
I have someone I feel safe sharing my deepest secrets with, even if it is myself.	True	Sometimes True	Sometimes False	False

The Step-by-Step Astrology Workbook

KEY TAKEAWAYS

Understanding and unpacking how you experience the 8th house of sex and death can help you have a deeper sense of how you experience change and transformation.

- ◆ The 8th house represents your attitude toward crises, comfort with taboo subjects, and relationship to your psyche. Understanding this part of your chart can give you insight into your personal growth journey and empower you to transform into your highest potential.

- ◆ The planets represent an aspect of your personality. Any planets located in the 8th house influence your psyche and support you in your path to personal transformation.

- ◆ An individual's psyche and relationship to death and sex are complex and unique to them. Taking time to journal on the themes of the 8th house, such as where you try to control situations and where you give your power away, can help empower you to understand the deepest parts of your psyche.

- ◆ Understanding the house placement of your 8th house ruler provides a deeper insight into your learnings about your relationship with power.

- ◆ Practicing being completely vulnerable and honest with yourself about your deepest secrets is the first step in healing and ultimately transforming yourself to reach your highest potential.

CHAPTER 12

THE 9TH HOUSE OF ASTROLOGY

THE HOUSE OF SPIRITUALITY

The 9th house is where you seek and experience new ways of life, differing philosophies, and unique perspectives, ultimately to determine your own truth. This is key to understanding your chart as a whole, as your desire to continue to learn, explore, and share with the world impacts how you experience and understand every area of life.

In this chapter, you will learn about the Sagittarius-ruled 9th house and how it governs religions, ideologies, belief systems, higher education, and philosophy. Using your birth chart, you will then move through five workbook exercises designed to help you navigate interpreting your chart through the 9th astrological house.

While you can study the general themes of the 9th house and have a good understanding of its meaning, because houses ground your lived experiences, only you can know exactly how this particular area of life shows up for you. The workbook exercises help focus you on what informs your higher self, worldview, and spiritual path, so that you can have a more precise understanding of how you currently experience your 9th house and also where you have room to continue learning and evolving.

THE INFLUENCE OF THE 9TH HOUSE

The 9th house is ruled by Sagittarius and represents higher education, international travel, publishing, belief systems, religion, ideologies, and philosophy. It is where you can find anything big and expansive. We are constantly learning, exploring, and seeking in this area of life, always in search of truth. Understanding your 9th house provides insight into what philosophies you subscribe to, providing a lens for how you see truth in all areas of your chart.

If you have planets in the 9th house, you are a lifelong learner always seeking an adventure. It is not unlikely that you have one or more higher education degrees or perhaps have traveled to multiple countries. You may have a serious case of wanderlust, but it is because you are curious about the world around you and enjoy experiencing the unique lifestyles and worldviews that make up different cultures.

At best, the 9th house is also where you share your discoveries. Part of the search for new knowledge and experiences is for the purpose of teaching. This is why the 9th house also represents publishing in all forms, such as books, journals, speaking events, and teaching at a high level.

Ultimately, the 9th house supports you in experiencing the outer world so that you can enhance your inner world and inner truths. Here, you are to expand your mind and learn about all possible ways to view the world to discern your ultimate truth.

YOUR BIRTH CHART

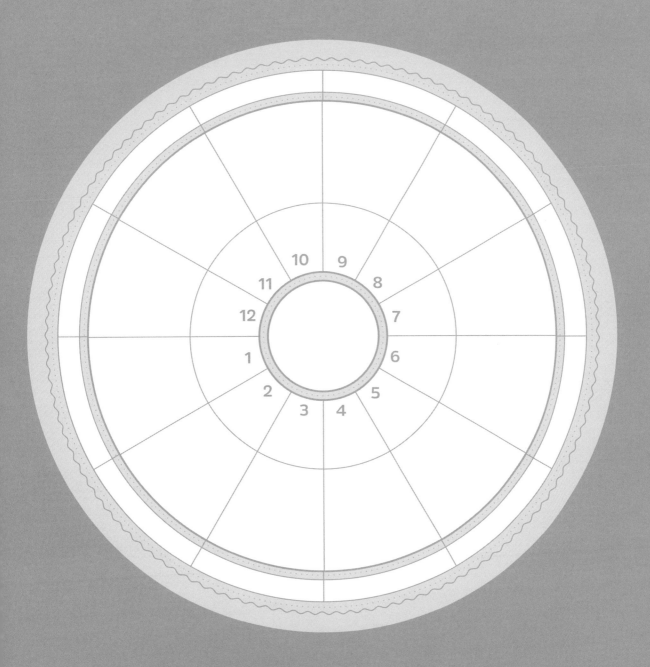

◯ EXERCISE 1

Although the 9th house is naturally ruled by Sagittarius, your personal birth chart will have a unique zodiac sign flavoring the energy of your 9th house. There may be one or more signs that take up space in your 9th house. The sign that is considered the ruler of your 9th house will be at the beginning of the house, closest to the 8th house and farthest from the 10th.

Fill in the four blanks at the end of this exercise by following these steps:

1. Review your birth chart to see what sign rules your 9th house. This is the sign that starts the house.

2. Use the table on page 42 to see what planet rules that particular sign. This is your 9th house ruling planet. Find that planet in your chart to see in which house it is located.

3. Use the table to determine the meaning of the house that holds your 9th house ruling planet.

The 9th house in my birth chart is ruled by _____ (sign). The sign that rules my 9th house is ruled by _____ (planet). The planet that rules my personal 9th house is located in the _____ (house) in my birth chart. This house represents _____ (house meaning). My belief systems also show up in this area of life. In this part of my chart, I have great potential for learning more about what I was taught to believe versus what I truly believe.

122   *The Step-by-Step Astrology Workbook*

☾ EXERCISE 2

This exercise will help you understand how your 9th house is influenced by your birth chart placements. In the first column of the following table, circle your 9th house planets. Then, read the correlating descriptions in the second column to see how you experience each planet.

9TH HOUSE PLANETS	9TH HOUSE EXPERIENCES
No planets in the 9th house	Review exercise 1 to learn which planet rules your 9th house. Find that planet in your birth chart. The sign that holds this planet will help you understand your 9th house.
Sun	You are a world traveler, or at least always seeking to explore. You are here to experience life and then share what you've experienced.
Moon	You are an emotional optimist and have an emotional need for exploration. Allow yourself to become immersed in feelings rather than running away from them.
Mercury	You are a truth teller and a student of life.
Venus	You love to learn. You value adventure and freedom.
Mars	You release energy through adventures and expressing your opinions.
Jupiter	You are constantly exploring and exchanging ideas, though you hold tightly to your own views.
Saturn	You may have grown up with rigid ideas imposed on you, and you are learning to speak your truth.
Uranus	You don't commit to or follow rules, and you have a deep need for freedom.
Neptune	You are open-minded and understand that there are many views to explore.
Pluto	You are passionate about learning and speaking your truth.

The 9th House of Astrology **123**

EXERCISE 3

The Sagittarius-ruled 9th house represents your belief systems and philosophies. The goal is to search for new knowledge through experience, coming away with your ultimate truth. This requires adventure, openness, and optimism. Use the journal prompts that follow to reflect on the themes of the 9th house.

1. What is spirituality? What does it mean to you?

2. Can you have a relationship with spirituality that is different from somebody else's sense of spirituality? How does a different understanding of spirituality make you feel?

3. What is truth? What does it mean to you?

4. Can there be more than one truth in a situation or topic? How do you feel when someone has a different truth or perspective on a situation or topic?

5. Have you ever thought something to be true and then changed your mind after learning or experiencing something new on the topic? How does that make you feel?

6. Do you actively share your truth with the world, or are you hiding part of it?

7. Is there anything you are running from? What happens when you confront it rather than running from it?

8. Write about the greatest adventure you've ever been on.

9. What could you talk about for one hour without any preparation? What would it feel like to share this with a larger audience?

10. Write a bucket list of at least ten items, none of which you've done before. What action can you take today to move toward at least one of these items?

124   *The Step-by-Step Astrology Workbook*

EXERCISE 4

In this exercise, you will learn the meaning of the placement of your 9th house ruler. In the following chart, identify your 9th house ruler and read the interpretation. For example, if your 9th house is ruled by Sagittarius, then your 9th house ruler is Jupiter, so look to see where Jupiter is in your chart. If you see Jupiter is in your 6th house, read the 6th house interpretation. Fill in the blanks:

My 9th house ruler is in the _____ (house). This means that I can learn about my exploration for truth and my belief system through _____ _____.

RULER OF THE 9TH HOUSE IS IN YOUR...	I CAN LEARN ABOUT MY EXPLORATION FOR TRUTH AND MY BELIEF SYSTEM THROUGH...
1st house	searching for my own identity.
2nd house	exploring my own set of values and resources.
3rd house	learning about my local community.
4th house	educating myself on my ancestral lineage and family history.
5th house	exploring creative pursuits.
6th house	determining what I believe it means to be responsible.
7th house	investigating what I learn about myself through relationships.
8th house	exploring my inner psyche.
9th house	traveling to new countries and learning about different belief systems.
10th house	understanding what type of legacy I want to leave behind.
11th house	determining what impact I want to have on humanity.
12th house	connecting to spirituality practices.

The 9th House of Astrology

EXERCISE 5

Respond to the statements in the following self-care checklist to discover whether you are in touch with the themes of the 9th house. If you answer mostly true, you likely already feel empowered in this area of your life. If you answer mostly false, it is nothing to stress about. It simply means you need to focus on this area of life more. It would also be helpful to lean into the qualities of the zodiac sign that is in this area of your chart. The journal prompts in exercise 3 on page 124 and this self-care checklist can support you in your journey of unpacking the themes of this house.

I have a clear sense of my spiritual beliefs.	True	Sometimes True	Sometimes False	False
I know what is true to me and I am not afraid to speak it.	True	Sometimes True	Sometimes False	False
I understand that different people will have different truths.	True	Sometimes True	Sometimes False	False
I use travel to experience new things, not to run away from my life.	True	Sometimes True	Sometimes False	False
I am constantly experiencing new things, even if it is in my own backyard.	True	Sometimes True	Sometimes False	False
I enjoy experiencing new cultures.	True	Sometimes True	Sometimes False	False
When I learn something new, I am not afraid to change my opinion.	True	Sometimes True	Sometimes False	False
I do not fear expressing my beliefs, even if it is a sensitive subject.	True	Sometimes True	Sometimes False	False

126   The Step-by-Step Astrology Workbook

KEY TAKEAWAYS

Understanding and unpacking how you experience the 9th house of spirituality can help you learn more about what is true to you.

- ◆ The 9th house represents philosophy, ideologies, belief systems, higher education, religion, publishing, and international travel. Understanding this part of your chart can help you experience the outer world so that you can discover your inner truths.

- ◆ The planets represent an aspect of your personality. Any planets located in the 9th house influence your worldview, educational style, interest in travel, and search for truth.

- ◆ An individual's educational path, worldview, and spiritual journey are complex and unique to them. Taking time to journal on the themes of the 9th house, such as your experience with education and your relationship with travel and adventure, can give more context to how you formed your worldview and how it may continue to evolve.

- ◆ Understanding the house placement of your 9th house ruler provides a deeper insight into your learnings about your ultimate truth.

- ◆ Writing a bucket list and taking action toward new adventures and then sharing your experiences with people around you can help you deepen your relationship with the themes of the 9th house.

CHAPTER 13

THE 10TH HOUSE OF ASTROLOGY

THE HOUSE OF AMBITION

The 10th house is the highest and most outward facing part of your chart, representing your career and higher calling. This is key to understanding your chart as a whole. What you feel inspired to pursue throughout your life, how you go about achieving these goals, and what impacts the balance of time and effort you spend in other areas of life can be found in the 10th house.

In this chapter, you will learn about the Capricorn-ruled 10th house and how it governs your career, ambitions, achievements, position in society, and contributions to humanity. Using your birth chart, you will then move through five workbook exercises designed to help you navigate interpreting your chart through the 10th astrological house.

While you can study the general themes of the 10th house and have a good understanding of its meaning, because houses ground your lived experiences, only you can know exactly how this particular area of life shows up for you. The workbook exercises help focus you on what informs your work ethic, long-term goals, and influence on society, so that you can have a more precise understanding of how you currently experience your 10th house and also where you may need more structure.

THE INFLUENCE OF THE 10TH HOUSE

The 10th house is ruled by Capricorn and represents your career, ambitions, position in society, and public reputation. It is where we feel purpose, expect high quality, and desire success. You are the CEO of your own life in this house, and it shows you where you work extra hard to achieve. While it is not your purpose on a soul level, it does give insight into your true calling from a public perception or career perspective.

It is the house right at the top of your chart. If you have planets in this house, there is a focus on status, fame, or public perception. People with several planets in the 10th house are typically successful in their careers and well respected for their achievements. Even if you don't have planets in the 10th house, you can identify what success means to you and discover a path that supports you in achieving it.

Although the Capricorn energy of the 10th house typically aligns with more traditional CEO-like success energy, your definition of and path to success will be unique. In the 10th house, you will learn what public role you choose, how you view success, and your relationship with power dynamics within the workplace or society.

Since the 10th house ultimately represents your role in society and how you are perceived by the public, it has a big impact on your reputation and legacy. In the 10th house, you can discover the impact you are meant to have on the world and what influence this will have beyond your time here.

YOUR BIRTH CHART

◯ EXERCISE 1

Although the 10th house is naturally ruled by Capricorn, your personal birth chart will have a unique zodiac sign flavoring the energy of your 10th house. There may be one or more signs that take up space in your 10th house. The sign that is considered the ruler of your 10th house will be at the beginning of the house, closest to the 9th house and farthest from the 11th.

Fill in the four blanks at the end of this exercise by following these steps:

1. Review your birth chart to see what sign rules your 10th house. This is the sign that starts the house.

2. Use the table on page 42 to see what planet rules that particular sign. This is your 10th house ruling planet. Find that planet in your chart to see in which house it is located.

3. Use the table to determine the meaning of the house that holds your 10th house ruling planet.

The 10th house in my birth chart is ruled by _____ (sign). The sign that rules my 10th house is ruled by _____ (planet). The planet that rules my personal 10th house is located in the _____ (house) in my birth chart. This house represents _____ (house meaning). How I appear publicly also shows up in this area of my chart, which can give me insight into how I am perceived in society.

132   The Step-by-Step Astrology Workbook

☾ EXERCISE 2

This exercise will help you understand how your 10th house is influenced by your birth chart placements. In the first column of the following table, circle your 10th house planets. Then read the correlating descriptions in the second column to see how you experience each planet.

10TH HOUSE PLANETS	10TH HOUSE EXPERIENCES
No planets in the 10th house	Review exercise 1 to learn which planet rules your 10th house. Find that planet in your birth chart. The sign that holds this planet will help you understand your 10th house.
Sun	You have great capacity to succeed and be a leader. You may have little privacy and your identity may be wrapped up in your public image.
Moon	You feel at home in the public eye and have an emotional need for achievement and recognition.
Mercury	You are naturally analytical and excel at structure and form.
Venus	You are tactful with your public image and are easily well received by others.
Mars	You put much of your energy toward your career and appear confident.
Jupiter	You have an expansive public image and are comfortable in public.
Saturn	You are learning to be the leader of your own life, and you take achievement very seriously.
Uranus	You carve out your own path to success and come across as quirky.
Neptune	A career that allows for freedom and intuition is important to you.
Pluto	You are obsessed with success and have the power to achieve it.

The 10th House of Astrology   **133**

EXERCISE 3

The Capricorn-ruled 10th house represents your career and public reputation. The goal is to find your unique path to success and understand the legacy you want to leave behind. For some, success may be equivalent to a financial status or job title; for others, it may be more related to family, friends, or self-development. Use the journal prompts that follow to reflect on the themes of the 10th house.

1.   What is success? What does it mean to you?

2.   Write about a time when you felt successful. What emotions were you experiencing? Was there a certain dollar amount, status, or public perception associated with the success?

3.   What is your relationship with authority figures? How can you be the authority of your own life?

4.   What is your top priority? What are you doing to show that you are actively committed to this priority?

5.   How are you perceived by the public? How do you feel about how you are perceived?

6.   Would you live your life differently if you didn't care about a certain public perception?

7.   What do you want to be remembered for? What are you actively doing right now to leave this impression behind?

8.   Are there parts of your life that you wish had more structure? How can you add structure to this part of your life?

9.   What is your greatest life aspiration? Have you done anything recently to move toward this goal?

10. List five long-term goals you want to achieve in the next five years. How will you know when you've achieved them?

EXERCISE 4

In this exercise, you will learn the meaning of the placement of your 10th house ruler. In the following chart, identify your 10th house ruler and read the interpretation. For example, if your 10th house is ruled by Cancer, then your 10th house ruler is the Moon, so look to see where the Moon is in your chart. If you see the Moon is in your 5th house, read the 5th house interpretation. Fill in the blanks:

My 10th house ruler is in the _____ (house). This means that I feel successful when I create structure around _____
_____.

RULER OF THE 10TH HOUSE IS IN YOUR...	I FEEL SUCCESSFUL WHEN I CREATE STRUCTURE AROUND...
1st house	my own priorities and physical body.
2nd house	my personal budget and material resources.
3rd house	my communication style and social activities.
4th house	my physical home and family.
5th house	my hobbies and the things I like to do for fun.
6th house	my day-to-day routines and health practices.
7th house	my partnerships and contracts.
8th house	my personal growth and transformation journey.
9th house	my education and travel pursuits.
10th house	my career and long-term goals.
11th house	my contribution to society and role in groups.
12th house	my spirituality practices.

EXERCISE 5

Respond to the statements in the following self-care checklist to discover whether you are in touch with the themes of the 10th house. If you answer mostly true, you likely already feel empowered in this area of your life. If you answer mostly false, it is nothing to stress about. It simply means you need to focus on this area of life more. It would also be helpful to lean into the qualities of the zodiac sign that is in this area of your chart. The journal prompts in exercise 3 on page 134 and this self-care checklist can support you in your journey of unpacking the themes of this house.

I know what success means to me, even if it is not the traditional version of success.	True	Sometimes True	Sometimes False	False
I am proud of my achievements, even if they are not textbook success.	True	Sometimes True	Sometimes False	False
I have a list of long-term goals and actively work toward them.	True	Sometimes True	Sometimes False	False
I am committed to my priorities in life.	True	Sometimes True	Sometimes False	False
I create structure when I feel lost.	True	Sometimes True	Sometimes False	False
I am confident in my public image and feel authentic in how I am perceived.	True	Sometimes True	Sometimes False	False
I know how to be the leader of my own life.	True	Sometimes True	Sometimes False	False
I feel purposeful and am confident in the legacy I am leaving behind.	True	Sometimes True	Sometimes False	False

The Step-by-Step Astrology Workbook

KEY TAKEAWAYS

Understanding and unpacking how you experience the 10th house of ambition can help you learn more about your true calling and public perception.

- ◆ The 10th house represents your career, ambitions, achievements, position in society, and public reputation. Understanding this part of your chart can help you understand more about your role in the workplace or society.

- ◆ The planets represent an aspect of your personality. Any planets located in the 10th house influence your work ethic, achievements, relationship with power dynamics, and how you view success.

- ◆ An individual's achievements and relationship with power dynamics are complex and unique to them. Taking time to journal on the themes of the 10th house, such as your relationship with authority figures, personal priorities, and life aspirations, can help you better understand your true calling.

- ◆ Understanding the house placement of your 10th house ruler provides a deeper insight into where you can create structure to feel successful.

- ◆ Writing a list of long-term goals that you want to achieve in the next five years can help you lean into the positive influences of the themes of the 10th house.

CHAPTER 14

THE 11TH HOUSE OF ASTROLOGY

THE HOUSE OF FRIENDSHIP

The 11th house is where you engage with society and humanity as a whole from a higher perspective. While this house has a focus on friends, it also encompasses the wider community. Understanding your 11th house is essential to creating an impact on humanity and ultimately learning how to take the power back to the people.

In this chapter, you will learn about the Aquarius-ruled 11th house and how it governs your friendships, social life, groups, technology, and humanitarian causes. Using your birth chart, you will then move through five workbook exercises designed to help you navigate interpreting your chart through the 11th astrological house.

While you can study the general themes of the 11th house and have a good understanding of its meaning, because houses ground your lived experiences, only you can know exactly how this particular area of life shows up for you. The workbook exercises help focus you on what informs how you show up as a friend, your humanitarian efforts, and your innovative capabilities, so that you can have a more precise understanding of how you currently experience your 11th house and also where you may need to more actively participate in community.

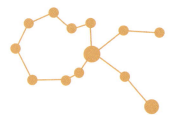

THE INFLUENCE OF THE 11TH HOUSE

The 11th house is ruled by Aquarius and represents friendship, innovation, technology, and humanitarian efforts. It is where we seek change beyond the status quo. The 11th house is where we think beyond ourselves to identify humanitarian challenges and create new ways of doing things to support real-time social issues.

As the house of friends and technology, the 11th house also rules all things social media and networking. Social media is a quintessential result of a strong 11th house. It is revolutionary in how it connects people far and wide, gives opportunity for new friends and connection, and has the capability to address humanitarian causes. Social media, like the 11th house, also represents social perception—how are you perceived by your friends, and how do you view them in turn? If you have planets in the 11th house, part of your purpose is to see people as they are, identify humanitarian challenges, and come up with innovative solutions that support the greater good.

Although the 11th house is focused on groups and communities, it is in the collective that you actualize your true self and define your role as an individual. Through friendships, networking, and group settings, you can learn more about your individual role in society and how you are here to uniquely support the greater good.

Ultimately, it is in the 11th house that we see the power in the collective. It is where the collective transcends traditional structures and systems that give the power to a few individuals and instead brings the power back to the people.

YOUR BIRTH CHART

◯ EXERCISE 1

Although the 11th house is naturally ruled by Aquarius, your personal birth chart will have a unique zodiac sign flavoring the energy of your 11th house. There may be one or more signs that take up space in your 11th house. The sign that is considered the ruler of your 11th house will be at the beginning of the house, closest to the 10th house and farthest from the 12th.

Fill in the four blanks at the end of this exercise by following these steps:

1. Review your birth chart to see what sign rules your 11th house. This is the sign that starts the house.

2. Use the table on page 42 to see what planet rules that particular sign. This is your 11th house ruling planet. Find that planet in your chart to see in which house it is located.

3. Use the table to determine the meaning of the house that holds your 11th house ruling planet.

The 11th house in my birth chart is ruled by _____ (sign). The sign that rules my 11th house is ruled by _____ (planet). The planet that rules my personal 11th house is located in the _____ (house) in my birth chart. This house represents _____ (house meaning). My contribution to humanitarian efforts also shows up in this area of my chart. I can learn more about my influence on society by understanding the 11th house.

142   The Step-by-Step Astrology Workbook

(EXERCISE 2

This exercise will help you understand how your 11th house is influenced by your birth chart placements. In the first column of the following table, circle your 11th house planets. Then read the correlating descriptions in the second column to see how you experience each planet.

11TH HOUSE PLANETS	11TH HOUSE EXPERIENCES
No planets in the 11th house	Review exercise 1 to learn which planet rules your 11th house. Find that planet in your birth chart. The sign that holds this planet will help you understand your 11th house.
Sun	You have social influence and are on a mission to innovate for the greater good of humanity.
Moon	You are intuitive and have an emotional need to belong.
Mercury	You think outside the box and have a quick mind.
Venus	You are a good networker and are aware of social etiquette and consequences.
Mars	You put energy into leading a community but not necessarily into being part of it.
Jupiter	You feel expansive in community and may take on leadership positions.
Saturn	You support groups by helping create structures and systems.
Uranus	You are here to create social change.
Neptune	You value groups but need to be careful not to lose your individuality.
Pluto	Even in balanced groups, you are aware of power dynamics.

The 11th House of Astrology   **143**

EXERCISE 3

The Aquarius-ruled 11th house represents your friendships, innovations, and humanitarian efforts. The goal is to actualize your true self by showing up in your collective role. This requires you to be uniquely you and let go of traditional structures. Use the journal prompts that follow to reflect on the themes of the 11th house.

1. What needs to be reformed in your life? What is no longer serving you and what new things can you implement that do serve you?

2. What are you doing because you were told to do it, even though it doesn't work for you? How can you change this?

3. What does friendship mean to you? How do your true friends make you feel?

4. What is your social circle like? Do you have a big group of friends, a few close friends, or something different? Do you feel fulfilled by this dynamic?

5. What is the most important thing that needs to be changed in society? What are you doing to help change this?

6. What is your relationship with technology? How are you using technology to your advantage?

7. Where is technology hindering you? Where do you need to use less technology?

8. What unique talents do you have? Are you sharing them with the world?

9. Are you collaborating with others? How can your strengths in combination with the strengths of others improve humanity?

10. Write a list outlining your vision for the future. What new ways of living exist? What old ways of living no longer exist?

EXERCISE 4

In this exercise, you will learn the meaning of the placement of your 11th house ruler. Below, identify your 11th house ruler and read the interpretation. For example, if your 11th house is ruled by Pisces, then your 11th house ruler is Neptune, so look to see where Neptune is in your chart. If you see Neptune is in your 12th house, read the 12th house interpretation. Fill in the blanks:

My 11th house ruler is in the _____ (house). This means that in friendship I am _____ and my humanitarian efforts are focused on _____.

RULER OF THE 11TH HOUSE IS IN YOUR...	IN FRIENDSHIP I AM _____. I FOCUS ON _____.
1st house	independent... helping people assert themselves
2nd house	resourceful... profitable and sustainable living
3rd house	communicative... creating community
4th house	nurturing... providing basic needs for others
5th house	playful... supporting children
6th house	practical... providing healthcare support for the community
7th house	other-oriented... creating harmony in community
8th house	sincere... psychological support for others
9th house	adventurous... widespread support and educating the community
10th house	pragmatic... supporting long-term goals
11th house	visionary... innovative solutions for humanity
12th house	sympathetic... connecting with spirituality

The 11th House of Astrology

EXERCISE 5

Respond to the statements in the following self-care checklist to discover whether you are in touch with the themes of the 11th house. If you answer mostly true, you likely already feel empowered in this area of your life. If you answer mostly false, it is nothing to stress about. It simply means you need to focus on this area of life more. It would also be helpful to lean into the qualities of the zodiac sign that is in this area of your chart. The journal prompts in exercise 3 on page 144 and this self-care checklist can support you in your journey of unpacking the themes of this house.

I have strong friendships and make an effort to stay connected with others.	True	Sometimes True	Sometimes False	False
I am skilled with technology and use it to my advantage.	True	Sometimes True	Sometimes False	False
I do not feel addicted to technology, and I intentionally spend time away from it.	True	Sometimes True	Sometimes False	False
I am sharing my uniqueness with the world in a productive way.	True	Sometimes True	Sometimes False	False
I collaborate with others who have strengths different from my own.	True	Sometimes True	Sometimes False	False
I don't do things just because I am told to; I do them because they feel authentic to me.	True	Sometimes True	Sometimes False	False
There are social issues I feel passionate about and am actively working to support.	True	Sometimes True	Sometimes False	False
I am active in my community.	True	Sometimes True	Sometimes False	False

The Step-by-Step Astrology Workbook

KEY TAKEAWAYS

Understanding and unpacking how you experience the 11th house of friendship can help you learn more about your group relationships and humanitarian efforts.

- ◆ The 11th house represents your friendships, social life, innovation, technology, and humanitarian efforts. Understanding this part of your chart can help you understand more about how you are here to uniquely support the greater good.

- ◆ The planets represent an aspect of your personality. Any planets located in the 11th house influence your impact in groups and society, your relationship with technology, how you innovate, and your impact on humanity.

- ◆ An individual's friendships and impact on humanity are complex and unique to them. Taking time to journal on the themes of the 11th house, such as your relationship with technology, your unique talents, your social circle, and your vision for the future, can help you learn how you can have the greatest impact on humanity.

- ◆ Understanding the house placement of your 11th house ruler provides a deeper insight into how you show up in friendship and what your humanitarian efforts are focused on.

- ◆ Writing a list outlining your vision for the future can have a positive influence on leaning into the themes of the 11th house.

CHAPTER 15

THE 12TH HOUSE OF ASTROLOGY

THE HOUSE OF SECRETS

The 12th house is the final house in your birth chart and is therefore where all other areas of life culminate. This is key to understanding your chart as a whole, as anything you hold on to and fear letting go in other areas of life is stored here in your subconscious. Here is where everything else from your chart goes to dissolve.

In this chapter, you will learn about the Pisces-ruled 12th house and how it governs your secrets, what is hidden beneath the surface, dreams, shadows, and intuition. Using your birth chart, you will then move through five workbook exercises designed to help you interpret your chart through the 12th astrological house.

While you can study the general themes of the 12th house and have a good understanding of its meaning, because houses ground your lived experiences, only you can know exactly how this particular area of life shows up for you. The workbook exercises help focus you on what informs your subconscious programming, innermost secrets, and anything you are hiding—even from yourself. This will help you have a more precise understanding of how you currently experience your 12th house and where you may need to set boundaries.

THE INFLUENCE OF THE 12TH HOUSE

The 12th house is ruled by Pisces and represents the subconscious, intuition, dreams, shadows, and what is hidden beneath the surface. This is the final house and therefore where everything culminates, only to then dissolve. As the house of endings, this is where you can identify what you may be holding on to from the previous eleven houses that needs letting go.

This area of the chart is karmic in nature, governing all things that exist without physical form, even giving us insight into past lives. It is an area in the chart where people disassociate or undo their relationship with physical reality. It can be challenging to discern past from present and real from imagined here.

The 12th house is where secrets are stored, even ones that the individual holding them may not be conscious of. Since there are no energetic boundaries here, it is possible this is where the individual is tangled in other people's secrets or energy. As a result, there is a deep need for solitude to differentiate this part of the subconscious from other individuals.

Spending time alone, meditating, or practicing being in a dream state can be supportive in transcending this part of the chart and reconnecting to your intuition. At worst, it is an area of caution, because some individuals are prone to addictive tendencies used to escape reality, such as drugs and alcohol. At best, it is where we fully process and integrate our secrets and fears, allowing us to be more sensitive and compassionate and have a desire to be of service to the collective.

YOUR BIRTH CHART

◯ EXERCISE 1

Although the 12th house is naturally ruled by Pisces, your personal birth chart will have a unique zodiac sign flavoring the energy of your 12th house. There may be one or more signs that take up space in your 12th house. The sign that is considered the ruler of your 12th house will be at the beginning of the house, closest to the 11th house and farthest from the 1st.

Fill in the four blanks at the end of this exercise by following these steps:

1. Review your birth chart to see what sign rules your 12th house. This is the sign that starts the house.

2. Use the table on page 42 to see what planet rules that particular sign. This is your 12th house ruling planet. Find that planet in your chart to see in which house it is located.

3. Use the table to determine the meaning of the house that holds your 12th house ruling planet.

The 12th house in my birth chart is ruled by _____ (sign). The sign that rules my 12th house is ruled by _____ (planet). The planet that rules my personal 12th house is located in the _____ (house) in my birth chart. This house represents _____ (house meaning). My shadow also shows up in this area of life. Since my shadow shows up in this area of life, I also have the greatest potential for developing depth and meaning here.

☾ EXERCISE 2

This exercise will help you understand how your 12th house is influenced by your birth chart placements. In the first column of the following table, circle your 12th house planets. Then read the correlating descriptions in the second column to see how you experience each planet.

12TH HOUSE PLANETS	12TH HOUSE EXPERIENCES
No planets in the 12th house	Review exercise 1 to learn which planet rules your 12th house. Find that planet in your birth chart. The sign that holds this planet will help you understand your 12th house.
Sun	You need alone time, but it is important that you know you don't need to go through life alone.
Moon	You are sensitive to collective energy. Boundaries and being able to self-nurture are both important to you.
Mercury	You are a dreamer and can easily channel ideas but may lack confidence in your communication.
Venus	You are a mystic at heart and should explore expressing yourself through art.
Mars	You need to release energy through spirituality and are learning how to stand up for yourself.
Jupiter	You unconsciously yearn to explore and break free.
Saturn	You likely had many responsibilities at a young age and unconsciously feel like you need to suffer in silence.
Uranus	You've been told to follow the rules but have an underlying urge to rebel.
Neptune	You are constantly daydreaming and would benefit from bringing your imagination to an art form.
Pluto	You may feel powerless, but you also feel passionate about the disempowered.

The 12th House of Astrology   **153**

EXERCISE 3

The Pisces-ruled 12th house represents your subconscious and what is hidden. The goal is to fully process and integrate any secrets or fears instilled in your subconscious, allowing you to be more compassionate and of service to the collective. Use the journal prompts that follow to reflect on the themes of the 12th house.

1. What do you spend the most time daydreaming about? How can you make this a reality?

2. Do you feel connected to your intuition? Do you trust your intuition? How can you listen to your intuition more?

3. Where are you self-destructive? What is the core belief you hold that causes this behavior? How can you transcend this belief?

4. What are you most fearful of? What experience in your life has caused you to be fearful of this? How can you let go of this fear?

5. Where can you add more magic into your life?

6. Have you ever experienced déjà vu? Write about the experience. What was your subconscious reminding you of?

7. What are you holding on to from any of the previous eleven houses? Do you need to keep this in your consciousness, or can you let it go?

8. When do you disassociate? What about that particular experience makes you not want to be present?

9. What tendencies do you use to escape reality? This could be alcohol, plant medicine, food, social media, television, shopping, or something else.

10. Where do you need to create more boundaries in your life? Why haven't you created these boundaries already? How is this affecting your connection to your intuition?

154   The Step-by-Step Astrology Workbook

EXERCISE 4

Now, you will learn the meaning of the placement of your 12th house ruler. Below, identify your 12th house ruler and read the interpretation. For example, if your 12th house is ruled by Taurus, then your 12th house ruler is Venus, so look to see where Venus is in your chart. If you see Venus is in your 3rd house, read the 3rd house interpretation. Fill in the blanks:

My 12th house ruler is in the _____ (house). This means that though I may feel isolated in this area of life, I have the greatest potential for developing depth and meaning by learning more about _____

_____.

RULER OF THE 12TH HOUSE IS IN YOUR...	THOUGH I MAY FEEL ISOLATED IN THIS AREA OF LIFE, I HAVE THE GREATEST POTENTIAL FOR DEVELOPING DEPTH AND MEANING BY LEARNING MORE ABOUT...
1st house	my own priorities and self-development.
2nd house	my financial security and self-worth.
3rd house	my local community and communication.
4th house	my home, legacy, and traditions.
5th house	my self-expression and creative work.
6th house	my service to others and personal health.
7th house	my relationships to others.
8th house	people in all stages of darkness and light.
9th house	philosophies, cultures, and belief systems.
10th house	my relationship with authority.
11th house	my friendships and how I can impact humanity.
12th house	how my beliefs point to something greater than me.

The 12th House of Astrology

EXERCISE 5

Respond to the statements in the following self-care checklist to discover if you are in touch with the themes of the 12th house. If you answer mostly true, you likely already feel empowered in this area of your life. If you answer mostly false, it is nothing to stress about. It simply means you need to focus on this area of life more. It would also be helpful to lean into the qualities of the zodiac sign that is in this area of your chart. The journal prompts in exercise 3 on page 154 and this self-care checklist can support you in your journey of unpacking the themes of this house.

I have dreams about my future.	True	Sometimes True	Sometimes False	False
I am actively working on unpacking the core beliefs that lead to self-destructive behaviors.	True	Sometimes True	Sometimes False	False
I see magic and beauty in everyday things.	True	Sometimes True	Sometimes False	False
Though I am empathetic and supportive of others, I have established solid boundaries.	True	Sometimes True	Sometimes False	False
When I feel the urge to escape reality, I instead use healthy coping mechanisms.	True	Sometimes True	Sometimes False	False
I have a strong connection to my spirituality.	True	Sometimes True	Sometimes False	False
I am actively learning what I have stored in my subconscious throughout my life.	True	Sometimes True	Sometimes False	False
When something no longer serves me, I have an ability to recognize that and let go.	True	Sometimes True	Sometimes False	False

KEY TAKEAWAYS

Understanding and unpacking how you experience the 12th house of secrets can help you learn more about what you've hidden beneath the surface in your subconscious.

- ◆ The 12th house represents your subconscious, shadow, intuition, dreams, and what is hidden beneath the surface. Understanding this part of your chart can help you unpack your subconscious and learn to trust your intuition more.

- ◆ The planets represent an aspect of your personality. Any planets located in the 12th house influence your shadow, subconscious, secrets, and intuition.

- ◆ An individual's secrets and subconscious programming are complex and unique to them. Taking time to journal on the themes of the 12th house, such as your connection with your intuition, your deepest fears, and tendencies to disassociate or escape reality, can help you develop depth and meaning and create healthier coping strategies.

- ◆ Understanding the house placement of your 12th house ruler provides a deeper insight into where you feel isolated in life but also have the power to find depth and meaning in your life.

- ◆ Establishing boundaries in your life is a good first step in supporting your connection to your intuition.

The 12th House of Astrology 157

A FINAL NOTE

Astrology is an ancient tool that uses the stars and changing seasons to give meaning to life cycles and human experiences. It has been used for centuries for self-reflection and to make major decisions. Though it can take a lifetime to learn the depths of astrology, simply by understanding the major players in astrology—zodiac signs, planets, and houses—every individual can have access to use astrology for self-reflection, personal growth, and preparing for their future.

The twelve houses in the birth chart, each representing an area of human life on Earth, help ground the planets and signs in your lived experiences. This book focuses on working through the twelve houses to help you understand your personality, how you experience each area of life, and what you can do to enhance or grow in each area of life.

Astrology teaches you to immerse yourself in your unconscious and encourages you to lean into your strengths and weaknesses to be the best version of yourself. As you better understand yourself, you may also find that you have greater compassion for the differences of others. The universe wants everyone to live their most authentic version of themselves, as it sees every individual as part of a whole. Using astrology, you have easy access to understanding your most authentic self. This knowledge leads to inner peace, the ability to align with the universe to live your highest path, and ultimately, if enough people lean into this ancient gift, a more harmonious and balanced collective.

RESOURCES

As you continue your journey to understand your birth chart and use astrology for personal growth, you may find these additional resources helpful:

The Only Astrology Book You'll Ever Need by Joanna Martine Woolfolk. In this book you'll find everything you need to know about planets, houses, and signs.

The Essential Guide to Practical Astrology by April Elliott Kent. This book gives a new understanding to basics by also addressing the more counterintuitive parts of astrology.

Chart Interpretation Handbook by Stephen Arroyo. Once you have the basics down, this book helps you put it all together to learn about others' charts.

Planets in Transit by Robert Hand. Your birth chart never changes, but the current planets always do. This book helps you understand how the current planets impact you.

You Were Born for This by Chani Nicholas. This book for radical self-acceptance goes in depth into your Sun, Moon, and rising signs.

Cafeastrology.com is a website where you not only can pull your birth chart for free but also can get basic birth chart interpretations, forecasts, and most basic astrology information.

Astro.com is a website where you can access your chart for free. It also has basic chart interpretations and an easy-to-use ephemeris for future predictions.

TimePassages is one of the best apps for having quick access to your own chart, including interpretations for current transits you are moving through.

Jessie Eccles has beginner, intermediate, and advanced astrology courses available on her website, as well as one-on-one consultations. Visit instagram.com/jessieeccles.

INDEX

A

Air signs, 17

Ambition, house of (10th), 129–137

Angles, 31

Aquarius, 15, 17, 18, 19, 20. *See also* 11th house (friendship)

Aries, 14, 17, 18. *See also* 1st house (self)

Ascendant (AC), 16, 31

Aspects, 31

Astrology

about, 4, 10, 158

constellation, 6–7

modern applications of, 5–6

myths and misconceptions about, 6–7

for personal growth, 7–9

Vedic, 4–5

Western (Tropical), 4–5

Authenticity, 8

B

Birth charts

about, 10, 23, 35

angles, 31

applying to your life, 33–34

apps for, 26, 28

aspects, 31

inner wheel, 32–33

outer wheel, 32–33

patterns in, 30

reading and interpreting, 27

significance of, 26–27

Bowl charts, 30

Bucket charts, 30

Bundle charts, 30

C

Cancer, 14, 17, 18. *See also* 4th house (home)

Capricorn, 15, 17, 18, 20. *See also* 10th house (ambition)

Cardinal signs, 18–19

Communication, house of (3rd), 59–67

Conjunction aspects, 31

Constellation astrology, 7

D

Death. *See* 8th house (sex & death)

Descendant (DC), 31

Dominant orientation, 20

E

Earth signs, 17

8th house (sex & death), 109–117

Elements, 17, 29

11th house (friendship), 139–147

F

5th house (pleasure), 79–87

Fire signs, 17

1st house (self), 39–47

Fixed signs, 19

4th house (home), 69–77

Free will, 33

Friendship, house of (11th), 139–147

Future, preparation for, 9

G

Gemini, 14, 17, 18, 19. *See also* 3rd house
(communication)

H

Health, house of (6th), 89–97

Home, house of (4th), 69–77

Horoscopes, 22, 23

Houses, 21, 23, 158. *See also specific*
  in the birth chart, 27, 29
  empty, 33
  in the inner wheel, 32
  stelliums in, 31–32

I

Imum coeli (IC), 31

Inner planets, 20

J

Jupiter, 20

K

Karma, 5

L

Leo, 14, 17, 18, 19. *See also* 5th house
(pleasure)

Libra, 14, 17, 18. *See also* 7th house
(relationships)

Locomotive charts, 30

Luminaries, 20

M

Mars, 20

Mercury, 20

Midheaven (MC), 31

Modalities, 18–19, 29

Moon, 20

Moon sign, 16

Mutable signs, 19

N

Neptune, 21

9th house (spirituality), 119–127

O

Opposition aspects, 31

Orientations, 19–20

Outer planets, 21

P

Personal signs, 19

Pisces, 15, 17, 18, 19, 20. *See also*
12th house (secrets)

Planets, 20–21, 23
  in the birth chart, 27, 28, 29
  stelliums, 29, 31–32

Pleasure, house of (5th), 79–87

Pluto, 21

Polarities, 17–18

R

Relationships, compatibility in, 9

Relationships, house of (7th),
99–107

Rising sign, 16, 31

S

Sagittarius, 15, 17, 18, 19, 20. *See also* 9th house (spirituality)
Saturn, 20
Scorpio, 14, 17, 18, 19. *See also* 8th house (sex & death)
2nd house (value), 49–57
Secrets, house of (12th), 149–157
Seesaw charts, 30
Self, house of (1st), 39–47
Self-discovery, 8
Self-reflection, 8
7th house (relationships), 99–107
Sex & death, house of (8th), 109–117
Sidereal system, 5
6th house (health), 89–97
Social planets, 20
Social signs, 19
Spirituality, house of (9th), 119–127
Splash charts, 30
Splay charts, 30
Square aspects, 31
Stelliums, 29, 31–32
Sun, 20
Sun sign, 4, 16. *See also* Zodiac signs

T

Taurus, 14, 17, 18, 19. *See also* 2nd house (value)
10th house (ambition), 129–137
3rd house (communication), 59–67
Transpersonal signs, 20
Trials, preparation for life's, 8

Trine aspects, 31
Tropic of Cancer, 5
Tropic of Capricorn, 5
12th house (secrets), 149–157

U

Uranus, 21

V

Value, house of (2nd), 49–57
Vedic astrology, 4–5
Venus, 20
Virgo, 14, 17, 18, 19. *See also* 6th house (health)

W

Water signs, 17
Wellness industry, 5
Western (Tropical) astrology, 4–5

Z

Zodiac signs, 4, 14–15, 23
  in the birth chart, 26–27, 28–29
  born on the cusp meaning, 15–16
  vs. constellations, 6
  elements associated with, 17
  modalities associated with, 18–19
  orientations associated with, 19–20
  in the outer wheel, 32
  planets associated with, 20–21
  polarities associated with, 17–18
  stelliums in, 32

ABOUT THE AUTHOR

 **Jessie Eccles** is an intuitive astrologer and educator. She believes that the universe has a way of guiding us forward through life and that astrology is a language we can use to better understand how the universe is supporting us. As an astrologer, her focus is to teach others how to open up their own potential, validate their unique gifts, find support through life's lessons, and come back to their own intuition. Her goal is to empower others to be the best version of themselves by using a practical approach for real-life results.

NOTES

NOTES